SELECTED POEMS

Selected Poems

by

A.E.

Swan River Press
Dublin, Ireland
MMXXII

Selected Poems
by A.E.

Published by
Swan River Press
Dublin, Ireland
in February MMXXII

www.swanriverpress.ie
brian@swanriverpress.ie

This edition © Swan River Press
"Poet, Seer and Scribe" © Daniel Mulhall

Cover design by Meggan Kehrli
from the portrait "A.E." by Count Casimir
Dunin Markiewicz, reproduced by permission from
Collection: Dublin City Gallery The Hugh Lane;

Set in Garamond by Ken Mackenzie

Published with assistance from Dublin UNESCO
City of Literature and Dublin City Libraries

Paperback Edition
ISBN 978-1-78380-762-8

Swan River Press published
a limited edition hardback of
Selected Poems in April 2017.

Contents

A Visionary xi
  W. B. Yeats

From *Homeward, Songs by the Way* (1894)

The Unknown God 7
By the Margin of the Great Deep . . . 8
The Hermit 9
The Great Breath 10
Sacrifice 11
Desire 12
Dusk 13
Night 14
Dawn 15
Day 16
Echoes 17
Parting 18
Oversoul 19
On a Hill-Top 20
Dust 21
Mystery 22
The Vesture of the Soul 23
Symbolism 24
The Dawn of Darkness 25
Sung on a By-Way 26
Three Counsellors 27

Indian	28
To One Consecrated	29
Natural Magic	30
Prayer	31
Oh, Be Not Led Away	32

From *The Earth Breath* (1896)

The Earth Breath	35
Immortality	37
The Mountaineer	38
Alter Ego	39
Divine Visitation	40
A Vision of Beauty	41
Love	43
Janus	44
In the Womb	45
The Memory of Earth	46
Duality	47
The Man to the Angel	48
Endurance	49
Illusion	51
Blindness	52
The Hour of Twilight	53
Content	54
The Gift	55

From *The Divine Vision* (1904)

The Divine Vision	59
Frolic	60
Refuge	61
A Summer Night	62
The Burning-Glass	64

Babylon	65
Remembrance	66
The Grey Eros	67
Night	69
Rest	70
The Voice of the Waters	71
The Twilight of Earth	72
Carrowmore	74
A Call of the Sidhe	76
The Master Singer	77
The Parting of Ways	78
A Farewell	80
Reconciliation	81

Poems 1903-1920

The Virgin Mother	85
Creation	86
The City	87
Continuity	89
Krishna	90
Reflections	92
On the Waters	93
In Memoriam	96
Recollection	97
An Irish Face	98
On Behalf of Some Irishmen Not Followers of Tradition	100
When	102

From *Voices of the Stones* (1925)

Outcast	105
Time	106

Artistry	108
Resurrection	109
Exiles	111
Promise	112
Mutiny	114
Night Wind	115
Wood Magic	116
Jealousy	118
Magnet	119
A Holy Hill	120
Transience	121
Unmeet	124
Forlorn	125
Momentary	126
The Lonely	127
A Prisoner	128
Michael	129

From *Vale and Other Poems* (1931)

Vale	143
The Gay	144
Blight	146
How?	147
Enchantment	149
Sibyl	150
Will o' the Wisp	152
"The Things Seen"	154
Midsummer Eve	155
Retribution	159
Ancestry	160
Germinal	161
Companions	163
Tirnanoge	164

Forgetfulness	165
Earth-Bound	166
The Cities	167
Atlantic	168
The Farewell of Pan	169

From *The House of the Titans* (1934)

Earth Spirit	173
Comfort	174
Lost Talisman	175
Two Magics	176
Incarnation	177
Karma	178
What Home	179
A Mountain Tarn	180
The Dark Lady	181
Dana	190
The Warrior of Heaven	192
A Farewell	194

✧

An Evening with A.E.	195
Edgar DeWitt Jones	
Poet, Seer and Scribe	205
Daniel Mulhall	
Selected Bibliography	215
Acknowledgments	219
About the Author	221

A Visionary

A young man came to see me at my lodgings the other night, and began to talk of the making of the earth and the heavens and much else. I questioned him about his life and his doings. He had written many poems and painted many mystical designs since we met last, but latterly had neither written nor painted, for his whole heart was set upon making his mind strong, vigorous, and calm, and the emotional life of the artist was bad for him, he feared. He recited his poems readily, however. He had them all in his memory. Some indeed had never been written down. They, with their wild music as of winds blowing in the reeds, seemed to me the very inmost voice of Celtic sadness, and of Celtic longing for infinite things the world has never seen. Suddenly it seemed to me that he was peering about him a little eagerly. "Do you see anything, X——?" I said. "A shining, winged woman, covered by her long hair, is standing near the doorway," he answered, or some such words. "Is it the influence of some living person who thinks of us, and whose thoughts appear to us in that symbolic form?" I said; for I am well instructed in the ways of the visionaries and in the fashion of their speech. "No," he replied; "for if it were the thoughts of a person who is alive I should feel the living influence in my living body, and my heart would beat and my breath would fail. It is a spirit. It is some one who is dead or who has never lived."

I asked what he was doing, and found he was clerk in a large shop. His pleasure, however, was to wander about upon the hills, talking to half-mad and visionary peasants, or to persuade queer and conscience-stricken persons to deliver up the keeping of their troubles into his care. Another night, when I was with him in his own lodging, more than one turned up to talk over their beliefs and disbeliefs, and sun them as it were in the subtle light of his mind. Sometimes visions come to him as he talks with them, and he is rumoured to have told divers people true matters of their past days and distant friends, and left them hushed with dread of their strange teacher, who seems scarce more than a boy, and is so much more subtle than the oldest among them.

The poetry he recited me was full of his nature and his visions. Sometimes it told of other lives he believes himself to have lived in other centuries, sometimes of people he had talked to, revealing them to their own minds. I told him I would write an article upon him and it, and was told in turn that I might do so if I did not mention his name, for he wished to be always "unknown, obscure, impersonal". Next day a bundle of his poems arrived, and with them a note in these words: "Here are copies of verses you said you liked. I do not think I could ever write or paint any more. I prepare myself for a cycle of other activities in some other life. I will make rigid my roots and branches. It is not now my turn to burst into leaves and flowers."

The poems were all endeavours to capture some high, impalpable mood in a net of obscure images. There were fine passages in all, but these were often embedded in thoughts which have evidently a special value to his mind, but are to other men the counters of an unknown coinage. To them they seem merely so much brass or copper or tarnished silver at the best. At other times the beauty of

A Visionary

the thought was obscured by careless writing as though he had suddenly doubted if writing was not a foolish labour. He had frequently illustrated his verses with drawings, in which an unperfect anatomy did not altogether hide extreme beauty of feeling. The faeries in whom he believes have given him many subjects, notably Thomas of Ercildoune sitting motionless in the twilight while a young and beautiful creature leans softly out of the shadow and whispers in his ear. He had delighted above all in strong effects of colour: spirits who have upon their heads instead of hair the feathers of peacocks; a phantom reaching from a swirl of flame towards a star; a spirit passing with a globe of iridescent crystal—symbol of the soul—half shut within his hand. But always under this largess of colour lay some tender homily addressed to man's fragile hopes. This spiritual eagerness draws to him all those who, like himself, seek for illumination or else mourn for a joy that has gone. One of these especially comes to mind. A winter or two ago he spent much of the night walking up and down upon the mountain talking to an old peasant who, dumb to most men, poured out his cares for him. Both were unhappy: X—— because he had then first decided that art and poetry were not for him, and the old peasant because his life was ebbing out with no achievement remaining and no hope left him. Both how Celtic! how full of striving after a something never to be completely expressed in word or deed. The peasant was wandering in his mind with prolonged sorrow. Once he burst out with "God possesses the heavens—God possesses the heavens—but He covets the world"; and once he lamented that his old neighbours were gone, and that all had forgotten him: they used to draw a chair to the fire for him in every cabin, and now they said, "Who is that old fellow there?" "The fret" (Irish for doom) "is over me," he repeated, and then went on to talk once more of God and heaven. More than once also he said, waving his arm towards the mountain, "Only myself knows what happened under the thorn-tree forty years ago"; and as he said it the tears upon his face glistened in the moonlight.

This old man always rises before me when I think of X——. Both seek—one in wandering sentences, the other in symbolic pictures and subtle allegoric poetry—to express a something that lies beyond the range of expression; and both, if X—— will forgive me, have within them the vast and vague extravagance that lies at the bottom of the Celtic heart. The peasant visionaries that are, the landlord duelists that were, and the whole hurly-burly of legends—Cuchulain fighting the sea for two days until the waves pass over him and he dies, Caolte storming the palace of the gods, Oisín seeking in vain for three hundred years to appease his insatiable heart with all the pleasures of faeryland, these two mystics walking up and down upon the mountains uttering the central dreams of their souls in no less dream-laden sentences, and this mind that finds them so interesting—all are a portion of that great Celtic phantasmagoria whose meaning no man has discovered, nor any angel revealed.

William Butler Yeats
The Celtic Twilight, 1893

Selected Poems

TO
Rose

If I should be remembered I would like it to be for the verses in this book. They are my choice out of the poetry I have written.
— A.E.

FROM
Homeward, Songs by the Way

TO
Charles Weekes

The Unknown God

Far up the dim twilight fluttered
    Moth-wings of vapour and flame:
The lights danced over the mountains,
    Star after star they came.

The lights grew thicker unheeded,
    For silent and still were we;
Our hearts were drunk with a beauty
    Our eyes could never see.

By the Margin of the Great Deep

When the breath of twilight blows to flame the misty skies,
All its vaporous sapphire, violet glow and silver gleam
With their magic flood me through the gateway of the eyes;
    I am one with the twilight's dream.

When the trees and skies and fields are one in dusky mood,
Every heart of man is rapt within the mother's breast:
Full of peace and sleep and dreams in the vasty quietude,
    I am one with their hearts at rest.

From our immemorial joys of hearth and home and love
Strayed away along the margin of the unknown tide,
All its reach of soundless calm can thrill me far above
    Word or touch from the lips beside.

Aye, and deep and deep and deeper let me drink and draw
From the olden fountain more than light or peace or dream,
Such primeval being as o'erfills the heart with awe,
    Growing one with its silent stream.

The Hermit

Now the quietude of earth
Nestles deep my heart within;
Friendships new and strange have birth
Since I left the city's din.

Here the tempest stays its guile,
Like a big kind brother plays,
Romps and pauses here awhile
From its immemorial ways.

Now the silver light of dawn,
Slipping through the leaves that fleck
My one window, hurries on,
Throws its arms around my neck.

Darkness to my doorway hies,
Lays her chin upon the roof,
And her burning seraph eyes
Now no longer keep aloof.

And the ancient mystery
Holds its hands out day by day,
Takes a chair and croons with me
By my cabin built of clay.

The Great Breath

Its edges foamed with amethyst and rose,
Withers once more the old blue flower of day:
There where the ether like a diamond glows
    Its petals fade away.

A shadowy tumult stirs the dusky air;
Sparkle the delicate dews, the distant snows;
The great deep thrills, for through it everywhere
    The breath of Beauty blows.

I saw how all the trembling ages past,
Moulded to her by deep and deeper breath,
Neared to the hour when Beauty breathes her last
    And knows herself in death.

Sacrifice

Those delicate wanderers,
The wind, the star, the cloud,
Ever before mine eyes,
As to an altar bowed,
Light and dew-laden airs
Offer in sacrifice.

The offerings arise:
Hazes of rainbow light,
Pure crystal, blue and gold,
Through dreamland take their flight;
And 'mid the sacrifice
God moveth as of old.

In miracles of fire
He symbols forth his days;
In gleams of crystal light
Reveals what pure pathways
Lead to the soul's desire,
The silence of the height.

Desire

With Thee a moment! Then what dreams have play!
Traditions of eternal toil arise,
Search for the high, austere and lonely way
The Spirit moves in through eternities.
Ah, in the soul what memories arise!

And with what yearning inexpressible,
Rising from long forgetfulness I turn
To Thee, invisible, unrumoured, still:
White for Thy whiteness all desires burn.
Ah, with what longing once again I turn!

Dusk

Dusk wraps the village in its dim caress;
Each chimney's vapour, like a thin grey rod,
Mounting aloft through miles of quietness,
    Pillars the skies of God.

Far up they break or seem to break their line,
Mingling their nebulous crests that bow and nod
Under the light of those fierce stars that shine
    Out of the calm of God.

Only in clouds and dreams I felt those souls
In the abyss, each fire hid in its clod;
From which in clouds and dreams the spirit rolls
    Into the vast of God.

Night

Heart-hidden from the outer things I rose;
The spirit woke anew in nightly birth
Unto the vastness where forever glows
    The star-soul of the earth.

There all alone in primal ecstasy,
Within her depths where revels never tire,
The olden Beauty shines: each thought of me
    Is veined through with its fire.

And all my thoughts are throngs of living souls;
They breathe in me, heart unto heart allied;
Their joy undimmed, though when the morning tolls
    The planets may divide.

Dawn

Still as the holy of holies breathes the vast,
Within its crystal depths the stars grow dim;
Fire on the altar of the hills at last
    Burns on the shadowy rim.

Moment that holds all moments; white upon
The verge it trembles; then like mists of flowers
Break from the fairy fountain of the dawn
    The hues of many hours.

Thrown downward from that high companionship
Of dreaming inmost heart with inmost heart,
Into the common daily ways I slip
    My fire from theirs apart.

Day

In day from some titanic past it seems
As if a thread divine of memory runs;
Born ere the Mighty One began his dreams,
    Or yet were stars and suns.

But here an iron will has fixed the bars;
Forgetfulness falls on earth's myriad races:
No image of the proud and morning stars
    Looks at us from their faces.

Yet yearning still to reach to those dim heights,
Each dream remembered is a burning-glass,
Where through to darkness from the Light of Lights
    Its rays in splendour pass.

Echoes

The might that shaped itself through storm and stress
In chaos, here is lulled in breathing sweet;
Under the long brown ridge in gentleness
    Its fierce old pulses beat.

Quiet and sad we go at eve; the fire
That woke exultant in an earlier day
Is dead; the memories of old desire
    Only in shadows play.

We liken love to this and that; our thought
The echo of a deeper being seems:
We kiss, because God once for beauty sought
    Within a world of dreams.

Parting

As from our dream we died away
Far off I felt the outer things:
Your wind-blown tresses round me play,
Your bosom's gentle murmurings.

And far away our faces met
As on the verge of the vast spheres:
And in the night our cheeks were wet,
I could not say with dew or tears.

O gate by which I entered in!
O face and hair! O lips and eyes!
Through you again the world I win
How far away from Paradise!

Oversoul

The East was crowned with snow-cold bloom
And hung with veils of pearly fleece:
They died away into the gloom,
Vistas of peace—and deeper peace.

And earth and air and wave and fire
In awe and breathless silence stood;
For One who passed into their choir
Linked them in mystic brotherhood.

Twilight of amethyst, amid
Thy few strange stars that lit the heights,
Where was the secret spirit hid?
Where was Thy place, O Light of Lights?

The flame of Beauty far in space—
Where rose the fire: in Thee? in Me?
Which bowed the elemental race
To adoration silently?

On a Hill-Top

Bearded with dewy grass the mountains thrust
Their blackness high into the still grey light,
Deepening to blue: far up the glimmering height
In silver transience shines the starry dust.

Silent the sheep about me; fleece by fleece
They sleep and stir not: I with awe around
Wander uncertain o'er the giant mound,
A fire that moves between their peace and peace.

The city myriads dream or sleep below;
Aloft another day has but begun:
Under the radiance of the Midnight Sun
The Tree of Life put forth its leaves to grow.

Wiser than they below who dream or sleep?
I know not; but their day is dream to me,
And in their darkness I awake to see
A Thought that moves like light within the deep.

Only from dream to dream our spirits pass;
Well, let us rise and fly from sphere to sphere;
Some one of all unto the light more near
Mirrors the Dreamer in its glowing glass.

Dust

I heard them in their sadness say,
"The earth rebukes the thought of God;
We are but embers wrapped in clay
A little nobler than the sod."

But I have touched the lips of clay,
Mother, thy rudest sod to me
Is thrilled with fire of hidden day,
And haunted by all mystery.

Mystery

Why does this sudden passion smite me?
I stretch my hands, all blind to see:
I need the lamp of the world to light me,
    Lead me and set me free.

Something a moment seemed to stoop from
The night with cool, cool breath on my face:
Or did the hair of the twilight droop from
    Its silent wandering ways?

About me in the thick wood netted
The wizard glow looks human-wise;
And over the tree-tops barred and fretted
    Ponders with strange old eyes.

The tremulous lips of air blow by me
And hymn their time-old melody:
Its secret strain comes nigh and nigh me:
    "Ah, brother, come with me;

"For here the ancient mother lingers
To dip her hands in the healing dew,
And lave thine ache with cloud-cool fingers
    Till sorrow die from you."

The Vesture of the Soul

I pitied one whose tattered dress
Was patched, and stained with dust and rain;
He smiled on me; I could not guess
The viewless spirit's wide domain.

He said, "The royal robe I wear
Trails all along the fields of light:
Its silent blue and silver bear
For gems the starry dust of night.

"The breath of Joy unceasingly
Waves to and fro its folds starlit,
And far beyond earth's misery
I live and breathe the joy of it."

Symbolism

Now when the spirit in us wakes and broods,
Filled with home yearnings, drowsily there rise
From its deep heart high dreams and mystic moods,
Mixing earth loves with its own native skies;
Clothing the vast with a familiar face;
Reaching its right hand forth to greet the starry race.

Wondrously near and clear the great warm fires
Stare from the blue; so shows the cottage light
To the field labourer whose heart desires
The old folk by the nook, the welcome bright
From the house-wife long parted from at dawn—
So the star villages in God's great depths withdrawn.

Nearer to Thee, not by delusion led,
Though there no house fires burn nor bright eyes gaze:
We rise, but by the symbol charioted,
Through loved things rising up to Love's own ways:
By these the soul unto the vast has wings
And sets the seal celestial on all mortal things.

The Dawn of Darkness

Come earth's little children pit-pat from their burrows on the hill;
Hangs within the gloom its weary head the languid daffodil.
In the valley underneath us through the fragrance flit along
Over fields and over hedgerows little quivering drops of song.
All adown the pale blue mantle of the mountains far away
Stream the tresses of the twilight flying in the wake of day.
Night comes; soon alone shall fancy follow sadly in her flight
Where the fiery dust of evening, shaken from the feet of light,
Thrusts its monstrous barriers between the pure, the good, the true,
That our weeping eyes may strain for, but shall never after view.
Only yester eve I watched with heart at rest the nebulae
Looming far within the shadowy shining of the Milky Way;
Finding in the stillness joy and hope for all the sons of men;
Now what silent anguish fills a night more beautiful than then:
For earth's age of pain has come, and all her sister planets weep,
Thinking of her fires of morning passing into dreamless sleep.
In this cycle of great sorrow for the moments that we last
We too shall be linked by weeping to the greatness of her past:
But the coming race shall know not, and the fount of tears shall dry,
And the arid heart of man be arid as the desert sky.
So within my mind the darkness dawned, and round me everywhere
Hope departed with the twilight, leaving only dumb despair.

Sung on a By-Way

What of all the will to do?
    It has vanished long ago,
For a dream-shaft pierced it through
    From the Unknown Archer's bow.

What of all the soul to think?
    Some one offered it a cup
Filled with a diviner drink,
    And the flame has burned it up.

What of all the hope to climb?
    Only in the self we grope
To the misty end of time:
    Truth has put an end to hope.

What of all the heart to love?
    Sadder than for will or soul,
No light lured it on above;
    Love has found itself the whole.

Three Counsellors

It was the fairy of the place,
Moving within a little light,
Who touched with dim and shadowy grace
The conflict at its fever height.

It seemed to whisper "Quietness,"
Then quietly itself was gone:
Yet echoes of its mute caress
Were with me as the years went on.

It was the warrior within
Who called "Awake, prepare for fight:
Yet lose not memory in the din:
Make of thy gentleness thy might:

"Make of thy silence words to shake
The long-enthroned kings of earth:
Make of thy will the force to break
Their towers of wantonness and mirth."

It was the wise all-seeing soul
Who counselled neither war nor peace:
"Only be thou thyself that goal
In which the wars of time shall cease."

Indian

Shadowy-petalled, like the lotus, loom the mountains with
    their snows:
Through the sapphire Soma rising such a flood of glory throws
As when first in yellow splendour Brahma from the Lotus rose.

High above the darkening mounds where fade the fairy
    lights of day,
All the tiny planet folk are waving us from far away;
Thrilled by Brahma's breath they sparkle with the magic
    of the gay.

Brahma, all alone in gladness, dreams the joys that throng
    in space,
Shepherds all the whirling splendours onward to their
    resting place,
Where in worlds of lovely silence fade in one the starry race.

To One Consecrated

Your paths were all unknown to us:
We were so far away from you:
We mixed in thought your spirit thus—
With whiteness, stars of gold, and dew.

The Mighty Mother nourished you;
Her breath blew from her mystic bowers;
Their elfin glimmer floated through
The pureness of your shadowy hours.

The Mighty Mother made you wise,
Gave love that clears the hidden ways;
Her glooms were glory to your eyes,
Her darkness but the fount of days.

She made all gentleness in you
And beauty radiant as the morn's:
She made our joy in yours, then drew
Upon your head a crown of thorns.

Your eyes are filled with tender light
For those whose eyes are dim with tears:
They see your brow is crowned and bright
But not its ring of wounding spears.

Natural Magic

We are tired who follow after
Phantasy and truth that flies:
You with only look and laughter
Stain our hearts with richest dyes.

When you break upon our study
Vanish all our frosty cares;
As the diamond deep grows ruddy,
Filled with morning unawares.

With the stuff that dreams are made of
But an empty house we build:
Glooms we are ourselves afraid of,
By the ancient starlight chilled.

All unwise in thought or duty—
Still our wisdom envies you:
We who lack the living beauty
Half our secret knowledge rue.

Thought nor fear in you nor dreaming
Veil the light with mist about;
Joy, as through a crystal gleaming,
Flashes from the gay heart out.

Pain and penitence forsaking,
Hearts like cloisters dim and grey,
By your laughter lured, awaking
Join with you the dance of day.

Prayer

Let us leave our island woods grown dim and blue;
O'er the waters creeping the pearl dust of the eve
Hides the silver of the long wave rippling through:
    The chill for the warm room let us leave.

Turn the lamp down low and draw the curtain wide,
So the greyness of the starlight bathes the room;
Let us see the giant face of night outside,
    Though vague as a moth's wing is the gloom.

Rumour of the fierce-pulsed city far away
Breaks upon the peace that aureoles our rest,
Steeped in stillness as if some primeval day
    Hung drowsily o'er the water's breast.

Shut the eyes that flame and hush the heart that burns:
In quiet we may hear the old primeval cry:
God gives wisdom to the spirit that upturns:
    Let us adore now, you and I.

Age on age is heaped about us as we hear:
Cycles hurry to and fro with giant tread
From the deep unto the deep: but do not fear,
    For the soul unhearing them is dead.

Oh, Be Not Led Away

    Oh, be not led away.
Lured by the colour of the sun-rich day.
    The gay romance of song
Unto the spirit life doth not belong:
    Though far-between the hours
In which the Master of Angelic powers
    Lightens the dusk within
The holy of holies, be it thine to win
    Rare vistas of white light,
Half-parted lips through which the Infinite
    Murmurs its ancient song,
Hearkening to whom the wandering starry throng
    Waken primeval fires,
With deeper rapture in celestial choirs
    Breathe, and with fleeter motion
Wheel in their orbits through the surgeless ocean.
    So hearken thou like these,
Intent on it, mounting by slow degrees,
    Until thy song's elation
Echoes the multitudinous meditation.

FROM
The Earth Breath

TO
W. B. Yeats

The Earth Breath

From the cool and dark-lipped furrows
    Breathes a dim delight
Through the woodland's purple plumage
    To the endless night.
Aureoles of joy encircle
    Every blade of grass
Where the dew-fed creatures silent
    And enraptured pass.
And the restless ploughman pauses,
    Turns and, wondering,
Deep beneath his rustic habit
    Finds himself a king;
For a fiery moment looking
    With the eyes of God
Over fields a slave at morning
    Bowed him to the sod.
Blind and dense with revelation
    Every moment flies,
And unto the Mighty Mother,
    Gay, eternal, rise
All the hopes we hold, the gladness,
    Dreams of things to be.
One of all thy generations,
    Mother, hails to thee.
Hail, and hail, and hail for ever,
    Though I turn again
From thy joy unto the human
    Vesture of pain.

I, thy child who went forth radiant
    In the golden prime,
Find thee still the mother-hearted
    Through my night in time;
Find in thee the old enchantment
    There behind the veil
Where the gods, my brothers, linger.
    Hail, forever, hail!

Immortality

We must pass like smoke or live within the spirit's fire;
For we can no more than smoke unto the flame return
If our thought has changed to dream, our will unto desire,
    As smoke we vanish though the fire may burn.

Lights of infinite pity star the grey dusk of our days:
Surely here is soul: with it we have eternal breath:
In the fire of love we live, or pass by many ways,
    By unnumbered ways of dream to death.

The Mountaineer

Oh, at the eagle's height
To lie i' the sweet of the sun,
While veil after veil takes flight
And God and the world are one.

Oh, the night on the steep!
All that his eyes saw dim
Grows light in the dusky deep,
And God is alone with him.

Alter Ego

All the morn a spirit gay
Breathes within my heart a rhyme,
'Tis but hide and seek we play
In and out the courts of time.

Fairy lover, when my feet
Through the tangled woodland go,
'Tis thy sunny fingers fleet
Fleck the fire dews to and fro.

In the moonlight grows a smile
Mid its rays of dusty pearl—
'Tis but hide and seek the while,
As some frolic boy and girl.

When I fade into the deep
Some mysterious radiance showers
From the jewel-heart of sleep
Through the veil of darkened hours.

Where the ring of twilight gleams
Round the sanctuary wrought,
Whispers haunt me—in my dreams
We are one yet know it not.

Some for beauty follow long
Flying traces; some there be
Seek thee only for a song:
I to lose myself in thee.

Divine Visitation

The heavens lay hold on us: the starry rays
Fondle with flickering fingers brow and eyes:
A new enchantment lights the ancient skies.
What is it looks between us gaze on gaze;
Does the wild spirit of the endless days
Chase through my heart some lure that ever flies?
Only I know the vast within me cries
Finding in thee the ending of all ways.
Ah, but they vanish; the immortal train
From thee, from me, depart, yet take from thee
Memorial grace: laden with adoration
Forth from this heart they flow that all in vain
Would stay the proud eternal powers that flee
After the chase in burning exultation.

A Vision of Beauty

Where we sat at dawn together, while the star-rich heavens shifted,
We were weaving dreams in silence, suddenly the veil was lifted.
By a hand of fire awakened, in a moment caught and led
Upward to the heaven of heavens—through the star-mists overhead
Flare and flaunt the monstrous highlands; on the sapphire coast of night
Fall the ghostly froth and fringes of the ocean of the light.
Many coloured shine the vapours: to the moon-eye far away
'Tis the fairy ring of twilight, mid the spheres of night and day,
Girdling with a rainbow cincture round the planet where we go,
We and it together fleeting, poised upon the pearly glow;.
Half our eyes behold the glory; half within the spirit's glow
Echoes of the noiseless revels and the will of Beauty go.
By a hand of fire uplifted—to her star-strewn palace brought,
To the mystic heart of beauty and the secret of her thought:
Here of yore the ancient Mother in the fire mists sank to rest,
And she built her dreams about her, rayed from out her burning breast:
Here the wild will woke within her lighting up her flying dreams,
Round and round the planets whirling break in woods and flowers and streams,
And the winds are shaken from them as the leaves from off the rose,

And the feet of earth go dancing in the way that beauty goes,
And the souls of earth are kindled by the incense of her breath
As her light alternate lures them through the gates of
 birth and death.
O'er the fields of space together following her flying traces,
In a radiant tumult thronging, suns and stars and myriad races
Mount the spirit spires of beauty, reaching onward to the day
When the Shepherd of the Ages draws his misty hordes away
Through the glimmering deeps to silence, and within the
 awful fold
Life and joy and love forever vanish as a tale is told,
Lost within the Mother's being. So the vision flamed and fled,
And before the glory fallen every other dream lay dead.

Love

When our glowing dreams were dead,
Ruined our heroic piles,
Something in your dark eyes said:
"Think no more of love or smiles."

Something in me still would say,
"Though our dreamland palace goes,
I have seen how in decay
Still the wild rose clings and blows."

But your dark eyes willed it thus:
"Build our lofty dream again:
Let our palace rise o'er us:
Love can never be till then."

Janus

Image of beauty, when I gaze on thee,
Trembling I waken to a mystery,
How through one door we go to life or death
By spirit kindled or the sensual breath.

Image of beauty, when my way I go;
No single joy or sorrow do I know:
Elate for freedom leaps the starry power,
The life which passes mourns its wasted hour.

And, ah, to think how thin the veil that lies
Between the pain of hell and paradise!
Where the cool grass my aching head embowers
God sings the lovely carol of the flowers.

In the Womb

Still rests the heavy share on the dark soil:
Upon the black mould thick the dew-damp lies:
The horse waits patient: from his lowly toil
The ploughboy to the morning lifts his eyes.

The unbudding hedgerows dark against day's fires
Glitter with gold-lit crystals: on the rim
Over the unregarding city's spires
The lonely beauty shines alone for him.

And day by day the dawn or dark enfolds
And feeds with beauty eyes that cannot see
How in her womb the mighty mother moulds
The infant spirit for eternity.

The Memory of Earth

In the wet dusk silver sweet,
Down the violet scented ways,
As I moved with quiet feet
I was met by mighty days.

On the hedge the hanging dew
Glassed the eve and stars and skies;
While I gazed a madness grew
Into thundered battle cries.

Where the hawthorn glimmered white,
Flashed the spear and fell the stroke—
Ah, what faces pale and bright
Where the dazzling battle broke!

There a hero-hearted queen
With young beauty lit the van:
Gone! the darkness flowed between
All the ancient wars of man.

While I paced the valley's gloom
Where the rabbits pattered near,
Shone a temple and a tomb
With the legend carven clear:

*"Time put by a myriad fates
That her day might dawn in glory;
Death made wide a million gates
So to close her tragic story."*

Duality

Who gave thee such a ruby flaming heart
And such a pure cold spirit? Side by side
I know these must eternally abide
In intimate war, and each to each impart
Life from its pain, in every joy a dart
To wound with grief or death the self-allied.
Red life within the spirit crucified,
The eyes eternal pity thee: thou art
Fated with deathless powers at war to be,
Not less the martyr of the world than he
Whose thorn-crowned brow usurps the due of tears
We would pay to thee, ever ruddy life,
Whose passionate peace is still to be at strife,
O'erthrown but in the unconflicting spheres.

The Man to the Angel

I have wept a million tears:
Pure and proud one, where are thine,
What the gain though all thy years
In unbroken beauty shine?

All your beauty cannot win
Truth we learn in pain and sighs:
You can never enter in
To the circle of the wise.

They are but the slaves of light
Who have never known the gloom,
And between the dark and bright
Willed in freedom their own doom.

Think not in your pureness there,
That our pain but follows sin:
There are fires for those who dare
Seek the throne of might to win.

Pure one, from your pride refrain:
Dark and lost amid the strife
I am myriad years of pain
Nearer to the fount of life.

When defiance fierce is thrown
At the god to whom you bow,
Rest the lips of the Unknown
Tenderest upon my brow.

Endurance

He bent above: so still her breath
What air she breathed he could not say,
Whether in worlds of life or death:
So softly ebbed away, away,
The life that had been light to him,
So fled her beauty leaving dim
The emptying chambers of his heart
Thrilled only by the pang and smart,
The dull and throbbing agony
That suffers still, yet knows not why.
Love's immortality so blind
Dreams that all things with it conjoined
Must share with it immortal day:
But not of this—but not of this—
The touch, the eyes, the laugh, the kiss,
Fall from it and it goes its way.
So blind he wept above her clay,
"I did not think that you could die.
Only some veil would cover you
Our loving eyes could still pierce through;
And see through dusky shadows still
Move as of old your wild sweet will."
Though all the worlds were sunk in rest
The ruddy star within his breast
Would croon its tale of ancient pain,
Its sorrow that would never wane.
Ah, immortality so blind,
To dream all things with it conjoined
Must follow it from star to star

And share with it immortal years.
The memory, yearning, grief, and tears,
Fall from it and it goes afar.
He walked at night along the sands,
He saw the stars dance overhead,
He had no memory of the dead,
But lifted up exultant hands
To hail the future like a boy,
The myriad paths his feet might press.
Unhaunted by old tenderness
He felt an inner secret joy—
A spirit of unfettered will
Through light and darkness moving still
Within the All to find its own,
To be immortal and alone.

Illusion

What is the love of shadowy lips
That know not what they seek or press,
From whom the lure for ever slips
And fails their phantom tenderness?

The mystery and light of eyes
That near to mine grow dim and cold;
They move afar in ancient skies
Mid flame and mystic darkness rolled.

O beauty, as thy heart o'erflows
In tender yielding unto me,
A vast desire awakes and grows
Unto forgetfulness of thee.

Blindness

Our true hearts are forever lonely:
A wistfulness is in our thought:
Our lights are like the dawns which only
Seem bright to us and yet are not.

Something you see in me I wis not:
Another heart in you I guess:
A stranger's lips—but thine I kiss not,
Erring in all my tenderness.

I sometimes think a mighty lover
Takes every burning kiss we give:
His lights are those which round us hover:
For him alone our lives we live.

Ah, sigh for us whose hearts unseeing
Point all their passionate love in vain,
And blinded in the joy of being,
Meet only when pain touches pain.

The Hour of Twilight

When the unquiet hours depart
And far away their tumults cease,
Within the twilight of the heart
We bathe in peace, are stilled with peace.

The fire that slew us through the day
For angry deed or sin of sense
Now is the star and homeward ray
To us who bow in penitence.

We kiss the lips of bygone pain
And find a secret sweet in them:
The thorns once dripped with shadowy rain
Are bright upon each diadem.

No riotous and fairy song
Allures the prodigals who bow
Within the home of law, and throng
Before the mystic Father now,

Where faces of the elder years,
High souls absolved from grief and sin,
Leaning from out ancestral spheres
Beckon the wounded spirit in.

Content

Who are exiles? As for me
Where beneath the diamond dome
Lies the light on hill or tree,
There my palace is and home.

Who are lonely lacking care?
Here the winds are living, press
Close on bosom, lips and hair—
Well I know their soft caress.

Sad or fain no more to live?
I have pressed the lips of pain;
With the kisses lovers give,
Ransomed ancient joys again.

Captive? See what stars give light
In the hidden heart of clay:
At their radiance dark and bright
Fades the dreamy king of day.

Night and day no more eclipse
Friendly eyes that on us shine,
Speech from old familiar lips
Playmates of a youth divine.

Come away, O, come away;
We will quench the heart's desire
Past the gateways of the day
In the rapture of the fire.

The Gift

I thought, beloved, to have brought to you
A gift of quietness and ease and peace,
Cooling your brow as with the mystic dew
    Dropping from twilight trees.

Homeward I go not yet; the darkness grows;
Not mine the voice to still with peace divine:
From the first fount the stream of quiet flows
    Through other hearts than mine.

Yet of my night I give to you the stars,
And of my sorrow here the sweetest gains,
And out of hell, beyond its iron bars,
    My scorn of all its pains.

FROM
The Divine Vision

TO
Hugh and Lota

The Divine Vision

This mood hath known all beauty, for it sees
O'erwhelmed majesties
In these pale forms, and kingly crowns of gold
On brows no longer bold,
And through the shadowy terrors of their hell
The love for which they fell,
And how desire which cast them in the deep
Called God too from His sleep.
Oh Pity, only seer, who looking through.
A heart melted like dew,
Seest the long perished in the present thus,
For ever dwell in us.
Whatever time thy golden eyelids ope
They travel to a hope;
Not only backward from these low degrees
To starry dynasties,
But, looking far where now the silence owns
And rules from empty thrones,
Thou seest the enchanted hills of heaven burn
For joy at our return.
Thy tender kiss hath memory we are kings
For all our wanderings.
Thy shining eyes already see the after
In hidden light and laughter.

Frolic

The children were shouting together
And racing along the sands,
A glimmer of dancing shadows,
A dovelike flutter of hands.

The stars were shouting in heaven,
The sun was chasing the moon:
The game was the same as the children's,
They danced to the self-same tune.

The whole of the world was merry,
One joy from the vale to the height,
Where the blue woods of twilight encircled
The lovely lawns of the light.

Refuge

Twilight, a timid fawn, went glimmering by,
    And Night, the dark-blue hunter, followed fast.
Ceaseless pursuit and flight were in the sky,
    But the long chase had ceased for us at last.

We watched together while the driven fawn
    Hid in the golden thicket of the day.
We, from whose hearts pursuit and flight were gone,
    Knew on the hunter's breast her refuge lay.

A Summer Night

Her mist of primroses within her breast
Twilight hath folded up, and o'er the west,
Seeking remoter valleys long hath gone,
Not yet hath come her sister of the dawn.
Silence and coolness now the earth enfold,
Jewels of glittering green, long mists of gold,
Hazes of nebulous silver veil the height,
And shake in tremors through the shadowy night.
Heard through the stillness, as in whispered words,
The wandering God-guided wings of birds
Ruffle the dark. The little lives that lie
Deep hid in grass join in a long-drawn sigh
More softly still; and unheard through the blue
The falling of innumerable dew,
Lifts with grey fingers all the leaves that lay
Burned in the heat of the consuming day.
The lawns and lakes lie in this night of love,
Admitted to the majesty above.
Earth with the starry company hath part;
The waters hold all heaven within their heart,
And glimmer o'er with wave-lips everywhere
Lifted to meet the angel lips of air.
The many homes of men shine near and far,
Peace-laden as the tender evening star,
The late home-coming folk anticipate
Their rest beyond the passing of the gate,
And tread with sleep-filled hearts and drowsy feet.
Oh, far away and wonderful and sweet
All this, all this. But far too many things

A Summer Night

Obscuring, as a cloud of seraph wings
Blinding the seeker for the Lord behind,
I fall away in weariness of mind.
And think how far apart are I and you,
Beloved, from those spirit children who
Felt but one single Being long ago,
Whispering in gentleness and leaning low
Out of its majesty, as child to child.
I think upon it all with heart grown wild.
Hearing no voice, howe'er my spirit broods,
No whisper from the dense infinitudes,
This world of myriad things whose distance awes.
Ah me; how innocent our childhood was!

The Burning-Glass

A shaft of fire that falls like dew,
    And melts and maddens all my blood,
From out thy spirit flashes through
    The burning-glass of womanhood.

Only so far; here must I stay:
    Nearer I miss the light, the fire.
I must endure the torturing ray,
    And with all beauty, all desire.

Ah, time long must the effort be,
    And far the way that I must go
To bring my spirit unto thee,
    Behind the glass, within the glow.

Babylon

The blue dusk ran between the streets: my love was winged within my mind,
It left to-day and yesterday and thrice a thousand years behind.
To-day was past and dead for me, for from to-day my feet had run
Through thrice a thousand years to walk the ways of ancient Babylon.
On temple top and palace roof the burnished gold flung back the rays
Of a red sunset that was dead and lost beyond a million days.
The tower of heaven turns darker blue, a starry sparkle now begins;
The mystery and magnificence, the myriad beauty and the sins
Come back to me. I walk beneath the shadowy multitude of towers;
Within the gloom the fountain jets its pallid mist in lily flowers.
The waters lull me and the scent of many gardens, and I hear
Familiar voices, and the voice I love is whispering in my ear.
Oh, real as in dream all this; and then a hand on mine is laid:
The wave of phantom time withdraws; and that young Babylonian maid,
One drop of beauty left behind from all the flowing of that tide,
Is looking with the self-same eyes, and here in Ireland by my side.
Oh, light our life in Babylon, but Babylon has taken wings,
While we are in the calm and proud procession of eternal things.

Remembrance

There were many burning hours on the heartsweet tide,
    And we passed away from ourselves, forgetting all
The immortal moods that faded, the god who died,
    Hastening away to the King on a distant call.

There were ruby dews were shed when the heart was riven,
    And passionate pleading and prayers to the dead we had wronged;
And we passed away, unremembering and unforgiven,
    Hastening away to the King for the peace we longed.

Love unremembered and heart-ache we left behind,
    We forsook them, unheeding, hastening away in our flight;
We knew the hearts we had wronged of old we would find
    When we came to the fold of the King for rest in the night.

The Grey Eros

We are desert leagues apart;
    Time is misty ages now
Since the warmth of heart to heart
    Chased the shadows from my brow.

Oh, I am so old, meseems
    I am next of kin to Time,
The historian of her dreams
    From the long-forgotten prime.

You have come a path of flowers:
    What a way was mine to roam!
Many a fallen empire's towers,
    Many a ruined heart my home.

No, there is no comfort, none.
    All the dewy tender breath
Idly falls when life is done
    On the starless brow of death.

Though the dream of love may tire,
    In the ages long agone
There were ruby hearts of fire—
    Ah, the daughters of the dawn!

Though I am so feeble now,
    I remember when our pride
Could not to the Mighty bow;
    We would sweep His stars aside.

Mix thy youth with thoughts like those—
    It were but to wither thee,
But to graft the youthful rose
    On the old and flowerless tree.

Age is no more near than youth
    To the sceptre and the crown.
Vain the wisdom, vain the truth;
    Do not lay thy rapture down.

Night

Burning our hearts out with longing
    The daylight passed:
Millions and millions together,
    The stars at last!

Purple the woods where the dewdrops,
    Pearly and grey,
Wash in the cool from our faces
    The flame of day.

Glory and shadow grow one in
    The hazel wood:
Laughter and peace in the stillness
    Together brood.

Down from the heaven its secrets
    Drop one by one;
Where time is for ever beginning
    And time is done.

There light eternal is over
    Chaos and night:
Singing with dawn lips for ever,
    "Let there be light!"

There too for ever in twilight
    Time slips away,
Closing in darkness and rapture
    Its shining day.

Rest

On me to rest, my bird, my bird:
    The swaying branches of my heart
Are blown by every wind toward
    The home whereto their wings depart.

Build not your nest, my bird, on me;
    I know no peace but ever sway:
O lovely bird, be free, be free,
    On the wild music of the day.

But sometimes when your wings would rest,
    And winds are laid on quiet eves:
Come, I will bear you breast to breast,
    And lap you close with loving leaves.

The Voice of the Waters

Where the Greyhound River windeth through a loneliness
   so deep,
Scarce a wild fowl shakes the quiet that the purple bog-
   lands keep:
Only God exults in silence over fields no man may reap.

Where the silver wave with sweetness fed the tiny lives of grass
I was bent above, my image mirrored in the fleeting glass,
And a voice from out the water through my being
   seemed to pass.

"Still above the waters brooding, spirit, in thy timeless quest;
Was the glory of thine image trembling over east and west
Not divine enough when mirrored in the morning
   water's breast?"

With the sighing voice that murmured I was borne to ages dim
Ere the void was lit with beauty breathed upon by seraphim,
We were cradled there together folded in the peace in Him.

One to be the master spirit, one to be the slave awoke,
One to shape itself obedient to the fiery words we spoke:
Flame and flood and stars and mountains from the primal
   waters broke.

I was huddled in the heather when the vision failed its light:
Still and blue and vast above me towered aloft the solemn height,
Where the stars like dewdrops glistened on the mountain
   slope of night.

The Twilight of Earth

The wonder of the world is o'er:
    The magic from the sea is gone:
There is no unimagined shore,
    No islet yet to venture on.
The Sacred Hazels' blooms are shed,
The Nuts of Knowledge harvested.

Oh, what is worth this lore of age
    If time shall never bring us back
Our battle with the gods to wage
    Reeling along the starry track.
The battle rapture here goes by
In warring upon things that die.

Let be the tale of him whose love
    Was sighed between white Deirdre's breasts,
It will not lift the heart above
    The sodden clay on which it rests.
Love once had power the gods to bring
All rapt on its wild wandering.

We shiver in the falling dew,
    And seek a shelter from the storm:
When man these elder brothers knew
    He found the mother nature warm,
A hearth fire blazing through it all,
A home without a circling wall.

The Twilight of Earth

We dwindle down beneath the skies,
    And from ourselves we pass away:
The paradise of memories
    Grows ever fainter day by day.
The shepherd stars have shrunk within,
The world's great night will soon begin.

Will no one, ere it is too late,
    Ere fades the last memorial gleam,
Recall for us our earlier state?
    For nothing but so vast a dream
That it would scale the steeps of air
Could rouse us from so vast despair.

The power is ours to make or mar
    Our fate as on the earliest morn,
The Darkness and the Radiance are
    Creatures within the spirit born.
Yet, bathed in gloom too long, we might
Forget how we imagined light.

Not yet are fixed the prison bars;
    The hidden light the spirit owns
If blown to flame would dim the stars
    And they who rule them from their thrones:
And the proud sceptred spirits thence
Would bow to pay us reverence.

Oh, while the glory sinks within
    Let us not wait on earth behind,
But follow where it flies, and win
    The glow again, and we may find
Beyond the gateways of the day
Dominion and ancestral sway.

Carrowmore

It's a lonely road through bogland to the lake at Carrowmore,
And a sleeper there lies dreaming where the water laps the shore;
Though the moth-wings of the twilight in their purples are unfurled,
Yet his sleep is filled with music by the masters of the world.

There's a hand as white as silver that is fondling with his hair:
There are glimmering feet of sunshine that are dancing by him there:
And half-open lips of faery that were dyed a faery red
In their revels where the Hazel Tree its holy clusters shed.

"Come away," the red lips whisper, "all the world is weary now;
'Tis the twilight of the ages and it's time to quit the plough.
Oh, the very sunlight's weary ere it lightens up the dew,
And its gold is changed and faded before it falls to you.

"Though your lover's heart be tender, a tenderer heart is near.
What's the starlight in her glances when the stars are shining clear?
Who would kiss the fading shadow when the flower-face glows above?
'Tis the beauty of all Beauty that is calling for your love."

Oh, the great gates of the mountain have opened once again,
And the sound of song and dancing falls upon the ears of men,

Carrowmore

And the Land of Youth lies gleaming, quick with rainbow light and mirth,
And the old enchantment lingers in the honey-heart of earth.

A Call of the Sidhe

Tarry thou yet, late lingerer in the twilight's glory:
Gay are the hills with song: earth's faery children leave
More dim abodes to roam the primrose-hearted eve,
Opening their glimmering lips to breathe some won-
    drous story.
Hush—not a whisper! Let your heart alone go dreaming.
Dream unto dream may pass: deep in the heart alone
Murmurs the Mighty One his solemn undertone.
Canst thou not see adown the silver cloudland streaming
Rivers of elfin light, dewdrop on dewdrop falling,
Star-fire of silver flames, lighting the dark beneath?
And what enraptured hosts burn on the dusky heath!
Come thou away with them for Heaven to Earth is calling.
These are Earth's voice—her answer—spirits thronging.
Come to the Land of Youth: the trees grown heavy there
Drop on the purple wave the starry fruit they bear.
Drink: the immortal waters quench the spirit's longing.
Art thou not now, bright one, all sorrow past, in elation.
Made young with joy, grown brother-hearted with the vast,
Whither thy spirit wending flits the dim stars past
Unto the Light of Lights in burning adoration.

The Master Singer

A laughter on the hills of air, a music in the trembling grass;
And one by one the words of light as music through my being pass:
"I am the sunlight in the heart, the silver moon-glow in the mind;
My laughter runs and ripples through the wavy tresses of the wind.
I am the fire upon the hills, the dancing flame that leads afar
Each burning-hearted wanderer, and I the dear and homeward star.
A myriad lovers died for me, and in their latest yielded breath
I woke in glory giving them immortal life though touched by death.
They knew me from the dawn of time: if Hermes beats his rainbow wings,
If Angus shakes his locks of light, or golden-haired Apollo sings,
It matters not the name, the land: my joy in all the gods abides:
Even in the cricket in the grass some dimness of me smiles and hides.
For joy of me the daystar glows, and in delight and wild desire
The peacock twilight rays aloft its plumes and blooms of shadowy fire,
Where in the vastness too I burn through summer nights and ages long,
And with the fiery-footed watchers shake in myriad dance and song."

The Parting of Ways

The skies from black to pearly grey
    Had veered without a star or sun:
Only a burning opal ray
    Fell on your brow when all was done.

Aye, after victory, the crown;
    Yet through the fight no word of cheer;
And what would win and what go down
    No word could help, no light make clear.

A thousand ages onward led
    Their joys and sorrows to that hour;
No wisdom weighed, no word was said,
    For only what we were had power.

There was no tender leaning there
    Of brow to brow in loving mood;
For we were rapt apart, and were
    In elemental solitude.

We knew not in redeeming day
    Whether our spirits would be found
Floating along the starry way,
    Or in the earthly vapours drowned.

Brought by the sunrise-coloured flame
    To earth, uncertain yet, the while
I looked at you, there slowly came,
    Noble and sisterly, your smile.

The Parting of Ways

We bade adieu to love the old;
    We heard another lover then,
Whose forms are myriad and untold,
    Sigh to us from the hearts of men.

A Farewell

Only in my deep heart I love you, sweetest heart.
    Many another vesture hath the soul; I pray
Call me not forth from this. If from the light I part
    Only with clay I cling unto the clay.

And ah! my bright companion, you and I must go
    Our ways, unfolding lonely glories, not our own,
Nor from each other gathered but an inward glow
    Breathed by the Lone One on the seeker lone.

If for the heart's own sake we break the heart, we may
    When the last ruby drop dissolves in diamond light
Meet in a deeper vesture in another day.
    Until that dawn, dear heart, goodnight, goodnight.

Reconciliation

I begin through the grass once again to be bound to
    the Lord;
    I can see, through a face that has faded, the face full
        of rest
Of the earth, of the mother, my heart with her heart
    in accord,
    As I lie 'mid the cool green tresses that mantle her breast
I begin with the grass once again to be bound to the Lord.

By the hand of a child I am led to the throne of the King
    For a touch that now fevers me not is forgotten and far,
And His infinite sceptred hands that sway us can bring
    Me in dreams from the laugh of a child to the song of a star.
On the laugh of a child I am borne to the joy of the King.

ns 1903-1920

TO
Helen Waddell

The Virgin Mother

Who is that goddess to whom men should pray,
But her from whom their hearts have turned away,
Out of whose virgin being they were born,
Whose mother nature they have named with scorn
Calling its holy substance common clay.

Yet from this so despised earth was made
The milky whiteness of those queens who swayed
Their generations with a light caress,
And from some image of whose loveliness
The heart built up high heaven when it prayed.

Lover, your heart, the heart on which it lies,
Your eyes that gaze and those alluring eyes,
Your lips, the lips they kiss, alike had birth
Within that dark divinity of earth,
Within that mother being you despise.

Ah, when I think this earth on which I tread
Hath borne these blossoms of the lovely dead,
And makes the living heart I love to beat,
I look with sudden awe beneath my feet
As you with erring reverence overhead.

Creation

As one by one the veils took flight,
The day withdrew, the stars came up.
The spirit issued pale and bright
Filling thy beauty like a cup.

Sacred thy laughter on the air,
Holy thy lightest word that fell,
Proud the innumerable hair
That waved at the enchanter's spell.

O, Master of the Beautiful,
Creating us from hour to hour,
Give me this vision to the full
To see in lightest things thy power.

This vision give, no heaven afar,
No throne, and yet I will rejoice
Knowing beneath my feet a star
Thy word in every wandering voice.

The City

Full of Zeus the cities: full of Zeus the harbours:
full of Zeus are all the ways of men.

What domination of what darkness dies this hour,
And through what new, rejoicing, winged, ethereal power
O'erthrown, the cells opened, the heart released from fear?
Gay twilight and grave twilight pass. The stars appear
O'er the prodigious, smouldering, dusky, city flare.
The hanging gardens of Babylon were not more fair
Than these blue flickering glades, where childhood in its glee
Re-echoes with fresh voice the heaven-lit ecstasy.
Yon girl whirls like an eastern dervish. Her dance is
No less a god-intoxicated dance than his,
Though all unknowing the arcane fire that lights her feet,
What motions of what starry tribes her limbs repeat.
I, too, firesmitten, cannot linger: I know there lies
Open somewhere this hour a gate to Paradise,
Its blazing battlements with watchers thronged, O where?
I know not, but my flame-winged feet shall lead me there.
O, hurry, hurry, unknown shepherd of desires,
And with thy flock of bright imperishable fires
Pen me within the starry fold, ere the night falls
And I am left alone below immutable walls.
Or am I there already, and is it Paradise
To look on mortal things with an immortal's eyes?
Above the misty brilliance the streets assume
A night-dilated blue magnificence of gloom
Like many-templed Nineveh tower beyond tower;
And I am hurried on in this immortal hour.

Mine eyes beget new majesties: my spirit greets
The trams, the high-built glittering galleons of the streets
That float through twilight rivers from galaxies of light.
Nay, in the Fount of Days they rise, they take their flight,
And wend to the great deep, the Holy Sepulchre.
Those dark misshapen folk to be made lovely there
Hurry with me, not all ignoble as we seem,
Lured by some inexpressible and gorgeous dream.
The earth melts in my blood. The air that I inhale
Is like enchanted wine poured from the Holy Grail.
What was that glimmer then? Was it the flash of wings
As through the blinded mart rode on the King of Kings?
O stay, departing glory, stay with us but a day,
And burning seraphim shall leap from out our clay,
And plumed and crested hosts shall shine where men have been,
Heaven hold no lordlier court than earth at College Green.
Ah, no, the wizardy is over; the magic flame
That might have melted all in beauty fades as it came.
The stars are far and faint and strange. The night draws down.
Exiled from light, forlorn, I walk in Dublin Town.
Yet had I might to lift the veil, the will to dare,
The fiery rushing chariots of the Lord are there,
The whirlwind path, the blazing gates, the trumpets blown,
The halls of heaven, the majesty of throne by throne,
Enraptured faces, hands uplifted, welcome sung
By the thronged gods, tall, golden, radiant, joyful, young.

Continuity

No sign is made while empires pass.
The flowers and stars are still His care,
The constellations hid in grass,
The golden miracles in air.

Life in an instant will be rent
Where death is glittering blind and wild—
The Heavenly Brooding is intent
To that last instant on Its child.

It breathes the glow in the brain and heart,
Life is made magical. Until
Body and spirit are apart
The Everlasting works Its will.

In that wild orchid that your feet
In their next falling shall destroy,
Minute and passionate and sweet
The Mighyt Master holds his joy.

Though the crushed jewels droop and fade
The Artist's labours will not cease,
And of the ruins shall be made
Some yet more lovely masterpiece.

Krishna

(Imitated from a fragment of the Vaishnava Scriptures.)

I paused beside the cabin door and saw the King of Kings at play,
Tumbled upon the grass I spied the little heavenly runaway.
The mother laughed upon the child made gay by its ecstatic morn,
And yet the sages spake of It as of the Ancient and Unborn.
I heard the passion breathed amid the honeysuckle scented glade,
And saw the King pass lightly from the beauty that he had betrayed.
I saw him pass from love to love; and yet the pure allowed His claim
To be the purest of the pure, thrice holy, stainless, without blame.
I saw the open tavern door flash on the dusk a ruddy glare,
And saw the King of Kings outcast reel brawling through the starlit air.
And yet He is the Prince of Peace of whom the ancient wisdom tells,
And by their silence men adore the lovely silence where He dwells.
I saw the King of Kings again, a thing to shudder at and fear,
A form so darkened and so marred that childhood fled if it drew near.
And yet He is the Light of Lights whose blossoming is Paradise,

Krishna

That Beauty of the King which dawns upon the seers'
   enraptured eyes.
I saw the King of Kings again, a miser with a heart
   grown cold,
And yet He is the Prodigal, the Spendthrift of the Heav-
   enly Gold,
The largesse of whose glory crowns the blazing brows
   of cherubim,
And sun and moon and stars and flowers are jewels scattered
   forth by Him.
I saw the King of Kings descend the narrow doorway
   to the dust
With all his fires of morning still, the beauty, bravery, and lust.
And yet He is the life within the Ever-living Living Ones,
The ancient with eternal youth, the cradle of the infant suns.
The fiery fountain of the stars, and He the golden urn
   where all
The glittering spray of planets in their myriad beauty fall.

Reflections

How shallow is this mere that dreams!
Its depth of blue is from the skies,
And from a distant sun the gleams
And lovely light within your eyes.

We deem our love so infinite
Because the Lord is everywhere,
And love awakening is made bright
And bathed in that diviner air.

We go on our enchanted way
And deem our hours immortal hours,
Who are but shadow kings that play
With mirrored majesties and powers.

On the Waters

Our boat drifts in the heart of heat,
In diamond dances plays the light;
Above the wave our glances meet
The warmest world of blue and bright.
At harmony are sky and sea;
Your face shines on me young and gay,
And life has given all to me
That heart could wish this happy day.

Yet I have grown so sudden old
Your laughter sounds afar. I seem
As one who wakening tries to hold
A figure that he loved in dream,
And feels it lost beyond recall
In worlds unconquerable; so I
Am in an instant rapt from all:
I might be veiled within the sky.

The clouds float in the seraph blue
And still I see the waters shine,
In tender tones a name comes to
A vanished self that once was mine.
They thrill me not, I know not how
The lips but late so sweetly kissed.
A love more ancient draws me now
To keep some immemorial tryst.

Is love unbounded then so high
The love that woke it may not win,

When grown to fulness it must fly
And seek its own immortal kin?
Who are my kinsmen in the vast?
And shall I in this soundless calm
Find recompense for all the past,
Be nearer unto what I am?

Have you like me behind the veil
A self so mystic and so cold,
And if we could each other hail
Would all the pallor glow to gold?
Speak, for although I have the sense
Of destinies about me piled
And yet unveiled magnificence,
I feel but as a little child:

Or one the grave no longer owns,
Whose spirit breaks above the sods,
Is overlooked from awful thrones
And crouches at the feet of gods,
Nor sees nor hears he with bowed head
The judgment of the shining ring,
Nor what high doom at length is said
And echoed back from king to king.

The doom is spoken. It may be
That I shall never more forget
In all my thoughts of thee and me
The maya wherein life is set,
This wizardry shall still pursue
All things we had found firm or fair,
Till life itself seem frail as dew
Or bubble glistening on the air.

On the Waters

Your eyes hold mine once more. Your face
Again allures. Oh, let us fly!
There is some magic in this place
Would mar the dream of You and I.
Come, let us bend unto the oar,
Pull swift, beloved, there may be
Safe home on that far glimmering shore;
Oh! fly from the enchanted sea!

In Memoriam

Poor little child, my pretty boy,
Why did the hunter mark thee out?
Wert thou betrayed by thine own joy?
Singled through childhood's merry shout?

And who on such a gentle thing
Let slip the Hound that none may bar,
That shall o'ertake the swiftest wing
And tear the heavens down star by star?

And borne away unto the night,
What comfort in the vasty hall?
Can That which towers from depth to height
Melt in Its mood majestical.

And laugh with thee as child to child?
Or shall the gay light in thine eyes
Drop stricken there before the piled
Immutable immensities?

Or shall the Heavenly Wizard turn
Thy frailty to might in Him,
And make my laughing elf to burn
Comrade of crested cherubim?

The obscure vale emits no sound,
No sight, the chase has hurried far:
The Quarry and the phantom Hound,
Where are they now? Beyond what star?

Recollection

Through the blue shadowy valley I hastened in a dream:
Flower rich the night, flower soft the air, a blue flower the stream
I hurried over before I came to the cabin door,
Where the orange flame-glow danced within on the beaten floor.
And the lovely mother who drooped by the sleeping child arose:
And I see how with love her eyes are glad, her face how it glows.
And I know all this was past ten thousand years away.
But in the Ever-Living yesterday is here to-day,
And the beauty made dust we cry out for with so much pain.
Unknown lover, I lived over your joy again.
Long dead maiden, your breasts were warm for the living head.
It is we who have passed from ourselves, from beauty which is not dead.
I know, when I come to my own immortal, I will find there
In a myriad instant all that the wandering soul found fair:
Empires that never crumbled, and thrones all glorious yet,
And hearts ere they were broken, and eyes ere they were wet.

An Irish Face

Not her own sorrow only that hath place
Upon yon gentle face.
Too slight have been her childhood's years to gain
The imprint of such pain.
It hid behind her laughing hours, and wrought
Each curve in saddest thought
On brow and lips and eyes. With subtle art
It made that little heart
Through its young joyous beatings to prepare
A quiet shelter there,
Where the immortal sorrows might find a home.
And many there have come;
Bowed in a mournful mist of golden hair
Deirdre hath entered there.
And shrouded in a fall of pitying dew,
Weeping the friend he slew.
The Hound of Ulla lies, with those who shed
Tears for the Wild Geese fled.
And all the lovers on whom fate had warred
Cutting the silver cord
Enter, and softly breath by breath they mould
The young heart to the old,
The old protest, the old pity, whose power
Are gathering to the hour
When their knit silence shall be mightier far
Than leagued empires are.
And dreaming of the sorrow on this face
We grow of lordlier race,

An Irish Face

Could shake the rooted rampart of the hills
To shield her from all ills,
And through a deep adoring pity won
Grow what we dream upon.

On Behalf of Some Irishmen Not Followers of Tradition

They call us aliens, we are told,
Because our wayward visions stray
From that dim banner they unfold,
The dreams of worn-out yesterday.
The sum of all the past is theirs,
The creeds, the deeds, the fame, the name,
Whose death-created glory flares
And dims the spark of living flame.
They weave the necromancer's spell,
And burst the graves where martyrs slept,
Their ancient story to retell,
Renewing tears the dead have wept.
And they would have us join their dirge,
This worship of an extinct fire
In which they drift beyond the verge
Where races all outworn expire.
The worship of the dead is not
A worship that our hearts allow,
Though every famous shade were wrought
With woven thorns above the brow.
We fling our answer back in scorn:
"We are less children of this clime
Than of some nation yet unborn
Or empire in the womb of time.
We hold the Ireland in the heart
More than the land our eyes have seen,
And love the goal for which we start

On Behalf of Some Irishmen . . .

More than the tale of what has been."
The generations as they rise
May live the life men lived before,
Still hold the thought once held as wise,
Go in and out by the same door.
We leave the easy peace it brings:
The few we are shall still unite
In fealty to unseen kings
Or unimaginable light.
We would no Irish sign efface,
But yet our lips would gladlier hail
The firstborn of the Coming Race
Than the last splendour of the Gael.
No blazoned banner we unfold—
One charge alone we give to youth,
Against the sceptred myth to hold
The golden heresy of truth.

When

When mine hour is come
Let no teardrop fall
And no darkness hover
Round me where I lie.
Let the vastness call
One who was its lover,
Let me breathe the sky.

Where the lordly light
Walks along the world,
And its silent tread
Leaves the grasses bright,
Leaves the flowers uncurled,
Let me to the dead
Breathe a gay goodnight.

FROM
Voices of the Stones

TO
Padraic Colum

Outcast

Sometimes when alone
At the dark close of day,
Men meet in outlawed majesty
And hurry away.

They come to the lighted house;
They talk to their dear;
They crucify the mystery
With words of good cheer.

When love and life are over,
And flight's at an end,
On the outcast majesty
They lean as a friend.

Time

At every heart-beat
Through the magic day
A lovely laughing creature
Ran away.
Where have they wandered,
The flock so gay?

I had but looked on them
And away they ran,
The exquisite lips untouched.
As they began
To part, Time swept them
On his caravan.

These new-born beauties
The tyrant took.
Their gaze was on mine
And mine forsook.
I could not stay even
One lovely look.

In what fold are they?
Could I pursue
Through the Everliving
And know anew
All those golden motions
That were you?

Time

Were beauty only
A day the same,
We could know the Maker
And name His name.
We would know the substance
Was holy flame.

Is there an oasis
Where Time stands still
Where the fugitive beauty
Stays as we will?
Is there an oasis
Where Time stands still?

Artistry

To bring this loveliness to be,
    Even for an hour, the Builder must
Have wrought in the laboratory
    Of many a star for its sweet dust.

Oh, to make possible that heart
    And that gay breath so lightly sighed:
What agony was in the art!
    How many gods were crucified!

Resurrection

Not by me these feet were led
    To the path beside the wave,
Where the naiad lilies shed
    Moonfire o'er a lonely grave.

Let the dragons of the past
    In their caverns sleeping lie.
I am dream-betrayed, and cast
    Into that old agony.

And an anguish of desire
    Burns as in the sunken years,
And the soul sheds drops of fire
    All unquenchable by tears.

I, who sought on high for calm,
    Into the Everliving find
All I was in what I am,
    Fierce with gentle intertwined;

Hearts which I had crucified
    With my heart that tortured them;
Penitence, unfallen pride—
    These my thorny diadem!

Thou wouldst ease in heaven thy pain,
    O, thou fiery, bleeding thing!
All thy wounds will wake again
    At the heaving of a wing.

All thy dead with thee shall rise,
    Dies Irae. If the soul
To the Everliving flies,
    There shall meet it at the goal.

Love that Time had overlaid,
    Deaths that we again must die—
Let the dragons we have made
    In their caverns sleeping lie.

Exiles

The gods have taken alien shapes upon them,
Wild peasants driving swine
In a strange country. Through the swarthy faces
The starry faces shine.

Under grey tattered skies they strain and reel there:
Yet cannot all disguise
The majesty of fallen gods, the beauty,
The fire beneath their eyes.

They huddle at night within low, clay-built cabins;
And, to themselves unknown,
They carry with them diadem and sceptre
And move from throne to throne.

Promise

Be not so desolate
Because thy dreams have flown
And the hall of the heart is empty
And silent as stone,
As age left by children
Sad and alone.

Those delicate children,
Thy dreams, still endure:
All pure and lovely things
Wend to the Pure.
Sigh not: unto the fold
Their way was sure.

Thy gentlest dreams, thy frailest,
Even those that were
Born and lost in a heart-beat,
Shall meet thee there.
They are become immortal
In shining air.

The unattainable beauty
The thought of which was pain,
That flickered in eyes and on lips
And vanished again:
That fugitive beauty
Thou shalt attain.

Promise

The lights innumerable
That led thee on and on,
The Masque of Time ended,
Shall glow into one.
It shall be with thee for ever
Thy travel done.

Mutiny

That blazing galleon the sun,
This dusky coracle I ride,
Both under secret orders sail,
And swim upon the selfsame tide.

The fleet of stars, my boat of soul,
By perilous magic mountains pass,
Or lie where no horizons gleam
Fainting upon a sea of glass.

Come, break the seals and tell us now
Upon what enterprise we roam:
To storm what city of the gods,
Or—sail for the green fields of home!

Night Wind

I love to think this fragrant air
    I breathe in the deep-bosomed night
Has mixed with beauty, and may bear
    The burden of a heart's delight.

This may have been the burning breath
    That uttered Deirdre's love. It may
Have been a note outlasting death
    As Sappho sang her heart away.

It may have fanned a joy so deep
    That Ilium must pay the price,
And under desert sand must sleep
    Heroes and towers in sacrifice.

And this rich air, it may have been,—
    To bring these dreams, so sweet a throng,—
Sighed by the lovely listening queen
    While Solomon had sung his song.

So it will take from me, from thee,
    Ere from our being it departs,
And keep for lovers yet to be
    All the enchantment of our hearts.

Wood Magic

From whence has flown this argosy of air
That o'er the forest dropped its merchandise,
Spilling a fire so rich, a wine so rare?
Through the long glade from russet floor to skies
Darkness and fire are revellers everywhere.
The leaves like gold and emerald butterflies
With myriad quiverings roof the forest glade.
    Around me where I lie
The orange flames race through the tattered shade
    Dazzling the downcast eye.

Downcast the eye; but not the heart within;
The aerial wine delights: the unblinding fire
Opens the ways, far past the leafy din
And revelry of light; by what desire
Borne onward through invisible gates to win
To that high region where unto one lyre,
Player by the Magian of the Beautiful,
    The starry feet keep time,
And these last hyacinths in shadows cool
    Echo with distant rhyme.

Distant! The wizard air has breathed away
The heaviness from earth. The sombre trees
To cloud change unimaginably; nay;
To fire, to mind. Ancestral images,
Ere that unfallen Eden had its day
Of yet undimmed forest and flower, these

Wood Magic

Living and lustrous and ethereal shapes
    I see with sight unblind,
In heavenly valleys or on glittering capes
    Glowed in the Magian's mind.

They fade: the forest flickers round me now:
Once more the incessant birth and death of light
On russet floor, green leaf and burnished bough
Dazzle. Yet still the visionary sight
Holds faintly, as these thicker airs allow,
A magic mist of dancers pale and bright,
A foam of golden faces from the spheres
    Beyond sun rise or set,
With eyes that had for long forgotten tears
    Or never had been wet.

Vanished the angelic trees and beings all!
The wood darkens: the wind has ceased to fan
The glade to flame. Oh, it was magical!
Can I recall? The blinding sunlight ran
Over the burning hyacinth to fall
Starry upon yon water. So began
The incantation of the light which brought
    Rapt face and fiery wing,
The Heaven of Heavens: a myriad marvel wrought
    And from so slight a thing!

Jealousy

Youth met within a garden
And youth to youth revealed
Time's loveliest hidden secrets,
Things that were dead and sealed;

What domes of ivory wonder
Rose in the golden race;
What heavens were fabled o'er them—
For some face like this face.

Youth roamed by shore and mountain
And its new wisdom told,
But sea and earth were silent,
Their lovely faces cold.

Magnet

I had sweet company
Because I sought out none,
But took who came to me,
All by the magnet drawn.
I had sweet company.
I had no dark friends but one.

They passed on and away,
The old lure had gone.
The partings all were gay.
By some new magic drawn
They went another way.
I had no heartache but one.

Because that in my heart
There lurked satyr or faun,
There was one could not depart
And one who must be gone.
While the faun crouched in the heart
There was one who must be gone.

A Holy Hill

Be still: be still: nor dare
    Unpack what you have brought,
Nor loosen on this air
    Red gnomes of your thought.

Uncover: bend the head
    And let the feet be bare;
This air that thou breathest
    Is holy air.

Sin not against the Breath,
    Using ethereal fire
To make seem as faery
    A wanton desire.

Know that this granite height
    May be a judgement throne,
Dread thou the unmoveable will,
    The wrath of stone.

Transience

Why does my fancy soon forsake
All that is perfect to the eye,
The ruffled silver of the lake,
The silent silver of the sky,
Its single star that is so shy,
That trembles like a golden fawn
Strayed from the blue and shadowy wood
Of night upon the twilight lawn:
Why is the heart so soon withdrawn?
Even on earth's last lovely brood
Of primroses it hardly dwells,
Though myriads, a tender mist,
Warm the pale green of chilly dells,
The aftershine of amethyst,
The glades of midnight overhead,
Where browse the flocks the fawn has led,
All glimmering, till they are laid
Folded in light which is their shade—
Did ever earth from its first prime
Move to a lovelier dance than this?
But yet I cannot keep in chime.
Swift as the whirling dervish is
My heart floats on a swifter tide.
As one upon a hurrying stream
Sees towers and forests as in a dream
Drift by him upon either side,
So do I see, and then I fly
From these to that they prophesy.

It is not that my heart is cold
To beauty, for my pulses beat
As bloom and odour jet their sweet
From tiny fountains in the mould,
And many rainbow trumpets blow;
But still my heart divines from these
How near are the Hesperides,
How rich to have this overflow
From sacred earth through common clay:
And all my being yearns to run,
To tread the meadows of the sun
And bask in that enchanted day.

The suns that rise, the suns that set,
Time's tidal waves of blue and gold
That roll from far ethereal seas,
Hill-land and forest, starlit pool,
Are images we soon forget,
And swiftest when most beautiful.
For when most beautiful we feel
That there is something they reveal,
Some lordlier being of their kind;
And beauty only meaneth this
And to the symbol we are blind.

The gifts that fortune brings, the kiss,
The lovely life, the heart unveiled,
Are images of heights unscaled.
And we adore while to our thought
Being with symbol seems enwrought,
Yet if we would the rapture stay,
The spirit is the open door
Through which the prisoner steals away.
Maybe there is a native shore

Transience

For us, for it, where we may find
A beauty stedfast to the mind,
Joy that will not so lightly stray
To join the maskers in the dance,
Eternity with Time at play.

Unmeet

No, it was not our own,
That high delight;
It came with grass and flowers,
As day and night,
A breath from heavenly powers
That still delight.

The innocents of earth,
Her grass, her flowers,
May mingle in the play
Of heavenly powers,
Who burned our life away
In what brief hours.

Forlorn

My wisdom crumbles.
I am as a lone child.
Oh, had I the heart now
My weeping were wild.

My palace dwindles
Thin into air:
The Ancient Darkness
Is everywhere:

But the heart is gone
That could understand,
And the child is dead
That had taken Its hand.

Momentary

What wizard at twilight
Made gay the light feet?
What Voice in their voices
Sounded so sweet?

Who caught the children
Into His dream,
To sway with the boughs
And curve with the stream?

One dance in one mind
Were clouds in the air,
The rapturous feet,
The flicker of hair.

Too soon it was over
The magical hour.
They parted like leaves
From a withering flower.

The twilight thickened:
The moon rose pale,
And they ran to their homes
By the hill or the vale.

The Lonely

Lone and forgotten
Through a long sleeping,
In the heart of age
A child woke weeping.

No invisible mother
Was nigh him there
Laughing and nodding
From earth and air.

No elfin comrades
Came at his call,
And the earth and the air
Were blank as a wall.

The darkness thickened
Upon him creeping,
In the heart of age
A child lay weeping.

A Prisoner

Brixton, September 1920

See, though the oil be low, more purely still and higher
The flame burns in the body's lamp. The watchers still
Gaze with unseeing eyes while the Promethean will,
The Uncreated Light, the Everlasting Fire,
Sustain themselves against the torturer's desire,
Even as the fabled Titan chained upon the hill.
Burn on, shine here, thou immortality, until
We too can light our lamps at the funeral pyre;
Till we too can be noble, unshakeable, undismayed
Till we too can burn with the holy flame, and know
There is that within us can conquer the dragon pain,
And go to death alone, slowly and unafraid.
The candles of God already are burning row on row:
Farewell, light-bringer; fly to thy fountain again.

Michael

A wind blew by from icy hills,
Shook with cold breath the daffodils;
And shivered as with silver mist
The lake's pale leaden amethyst.
It pinched the barely budded trees
And rent the twilight tapestries:
Left for one hallowed instant bare
A single star in lonely air
O'er rocky fields the bitter wind
Had swept of all their human kind.

Ere that the fisher folk were all
Snug under thatch and sheltering wall,
Breathing the cabin's air of gold,
Safe from the blue storm and nipping cold.
And, clustered round the hearth within
With fiery hands and burnished chin,
They sat and listened to old tales
Or legends of gigantic gales.
Some told of phantom craft they knew
That sailed with a flame-coloured crew,
And came up strangely through the wind
Havens invisible to find
By those rare cities poets sung
Cresting the Islands of the Young.

How do the heights above our head,
The depths below the water spread,
Waken the spirit in such wise

That to the deep the deep replies,
And in far spaces of the soul
The oceans stir, the heavens roll?

Michael must leave the morrow morn
The countryside where he was born,
And all day long had Michael clung
Unto the kin he lived among.
But at some talk of sea and sky
He heard an older mother cry.
The cabin's golden air grew dim:
The cabin's walls drew down on him:
The cabin's rafters hid from sight
The cloudy roof-tree of the night.
And Michael could not leave behind
His kinsmen of the wave and wind
Without farewell. The path he took
Ran like a twisted, shining brook,
Speckled with stones and ruts and rills,
Mid a low valley of dark hills,
And trees so tempest bowed that they
Seemed to seek double root in clay.

At last the dropping valley turned:
A sky of murky citron burned,
Above through flying purples seen
Lay pools of heavenly blue and green.
From the sea rim unto the caves
Rolled on a mammoth herd of waves.
And all about the rocky bay
Leaped up grey forests of wild spray,
Glooming above the ledges brown
Ere their pale drift came drenching down.

Michael

Things delicate and dewy clung
To Michael's cheeks. The salt air stung.
From crag to crag did Michael leap
Until he overhung the deep;
Saw in vast caves the waters roam,
The ceaseless ecstasy of form,
Whirlpools of opal, lace of light
Strewn over quivering malachite,
Ice-tinted mounds of water rise,
Glinting as with a million eyes,
Reel in and out of light and shade,
Show depths of ivory or jade,
New broidery every instant wear
Spun by the magic weaver, Air.

Then Michael's gaze was turned from these
Unto the far, rejoicing seas
Whose twilight legions onward rolled
A turbulence of dusky gold,
A dim magnificence of froth,
A thunder tone which was not wrath,
But such a speech as earth might cry
Unto far kinsmen in the sky.
The spray was tossed aloft in air:
A bird was flying here and there.
Foam, bird and twilight to the boy
Seemed to be but a single joy.
He closed his eyes that he might be
Alone with all that ecstasy.

What was it unto Michael gave
This joy, the life of earth and wave?
Or did his candle shine so bright
But by its own and natural light?

Ah, who can answer for what powers
Are with us in the secret hours!
Though wind and wave cried out no less,
Entranced unto forgetfulness,
He heard no more the water's din;
A golden ocean rocked within,
A boat of bronze and crystal wrought
And steered by the enchanter, Thought,
Was flying with him fast and far
To isles that glimmered, each a star
Hung low upon the distant rim,
And then the vision rushed on him.

The palaces of light were there
With towers that faded up in air,
With amethyst and silver spires,
And casements lit with precious fires,
And mythic forms with wings outspread
And faces from which light was shed
High upon gleaming pillars set
On turret and on parapet.
The bells were chiming all around
And the sweet air was drunk with sound.

Too swift did Michael pass to see
Ildathach's mystic chivalry
Graved on the walls, its queens and kings
Girt round with eyes and stars and wings.
The magic boat with Michael drew
To some deep being that he knew,
Some mystery that to the wise
It clouded o'er by Paradise
Some will that would not let him stay
Hurried the boat away, away.

Michael

At last its fiery wings were still
Folded beneath some heavenly hill.
But was that Michael light as air
Was travelling up the mighty stair?
Or had impetuous desire
Woven for him that form of fire
Which with no less a light did shine
Than those with countenance divine
Who thronged the gateway as he came,
Faces to rapture and of flame,
The glowing, deep, unwavering eyes
Of those eternity makes wise.
And lofty things to him were said
As to one risen from the dead.

What there beyond the gate befell
Michael could never after tell.
Imagination still would fail
Some height too infinite to scale,
Some being too profound to scan,
Some time too limitless to span.
Yet when he lifted up his eyes
That foam was grey against the skies.
That same wild bird was on the wing.
That twilight wave was glimmering.
And twilight wave and foam and bird
Had hardly in his vision stirred
Since he had closed his eyes to be
Of that majestic company.

And can a second then suffice
To hurry us to Paradise,
What seemed so endlessly sublime
Shrink to a particle of time?

Selected Poems

Why was the call on Michael made?
What charge was on his spirit laid?
And could the way for him be sure
Made by excess of light obscure?
However fiery is the dream,
How faint in life the echoing gleam!
And faint was all that happed that day
As home he went his dreamy way.

And now had Michael, for his share
Of life, the city's dingy air,
By the black reek of chimneys smudged
O'er the dark warehouse where he drudged,
Where for dull life men pay in toll
Toil and the shining of the soul.
Within his attic he would fret
Like a wild creature in a net,
And on the darkness he would make
The jewel of the little lake,
A bloom of fairy blue amid
The bronze and purple heather hid;
Make battlemented cliffs grow red
Where the last rose of day was shed,
Be later in rich darkness seen
Against a sky of glowing green.
Or he would climb where quiet fills
With dream the shepherd on the hills,
Where he could see as from high land
The golden sickle of the sand
Curving around the bay to where
The granite cliffs were worn by air,
And watch the wind and waves at play,

Michael

The heavenly gleam of falling spray.
The sunlit surges foam below
In wrinklings as of liquid snow.
And he could breathe the airs that blew
From worlds invisible he knew.
How far away now from the boy!
How unassailable their joy!

So Michael would recall each place
As lovers a remembered face.
But, though the tender may not tire,
Memory is but a fading fire.
And Michael's might have sunken low,
Changed to grey ash its coloured glow,
Did not upon his hearing fall
The mountain speech of Donegal,
And that he swiftly turned to greet
The tongue whose accent was so sweet,
And found one of that eager kind
The army of the Gaelic mind,
Still holding through the Iron Age
The spiritual heritage,
The story from the gods that ran
Through many a cycle down to man.
And soon with them had Michael read
The legend of the famous dead,
From him who with his single sword
Stayed a great army at the ford,
Down to the vagrant poets, those
Who gave their hearts to the Dark Rose,
And of the wanderers who set sail
And found a lordlier Innisfail,

And saw a sun that never set
And all their hearts' desires were met.

How may the past if it be dead
Its light within the living shed?
Or does the Everliving hold
Earth's memories from the Age of Gold?
And are our dreams, ardours and fires
But ancient unfulfilled desires?
And do they shine within our clay
And do they urge us on their way?
As Michael read the Gaelic scroll
It seemed the story of the soul,
And those who wrought, lest there should fail
From earth the legend of the Gael,
Seemed warriors of Eternal Mind,
Still holding in a world grown blind,
From which belief and hope had gone,
The lovely magic of its dawn.

Thrice on the wheel of time recurred
The season of the risen Lord
Since Michael left his home behind
And faced the chilly Easter wind,
And saw the twilight waters gleam
And dreamed an unremembered dream.
Was it because the Easter time
With mystic nature was in chime
That memory was roused from sleep,
Or was deep calling unto deep?
The lord in man had risen here,
From the dark sepulchre of fear,
Was laughing, gay and undismayed,
Though on a fragile barricade

Michael

The bullet rang, the death star broke,
The street waved dizzily in smoke,
And there the fierce and lovely breath
Of flame in the grey mist was death.

Yet Michael felt within him rise
The rapture that is sacrifice.
What miracle was wrought on him
So that each leaden freighted limb
Seemed lit with fire, seemed light as air?
How came upon him dying there
Amid the city's burning piles
The vision of the mystic isles?
For underneath and through the smoke
A glint of golden waters broke;
And floating on that phantom tide
With fiery wings expanded wide
A barque of bronze and crystal wrought
Called forth by the enchanter, Thought.
And noble faces glowed above,
Faces of ecstasy and love,
And eyes whose shining calm and pure
Was in eternity secure,
And lofty forms of burnished air
Stood on the deck by Michael there.
And spirit upon spirit gazed.
Then one to Michael's lips upraised
A cup filled from that holy well
O'er which the Nuts of Wisdom fell,
And as he drank there reeled away
Vision of earth and night and day,
And he was far away from these
Afloat upon the heavenly seas.

I do not know if such a band
Came from the Many Coloured Land
Or whether in our being we
Make such a magic phantasy
Of images which draw us hence
Unto our own magnificence.
Yet many a one a tryst has kept
With the immortal while he slept,
Woke unremembering, went his way,
Life seemed the same from day to day,
Till the predestined hour came,
A hidden will leaped up in flame,
And through its deed the risen soul
Strides on self-conquering to the goal.

This was the dream of one who died
For country, said his countryside.
We choose this cause or that, but still
The Everlasting works Its will.
The slayer and the slain may be
Knit in a secret harmony.
What does the spirit urge us to?
Some sacrifice that may undo
The bonds that hold us to the clay
And limit life to this cold day?
Some for a gentle dream will die:
Some for an empire's majesty:
Some for a loftier humankind,
Some to be free as cloud or wind,
Will leave their valley, climb their slope.
Whate'er the deed, whate'er the hope,
Through all the varied battle-cries
A Shepherd with a single voice

Michael

Still lures us nigh the Gates of Gold
That open to the starry fold.

So may it be that Michael died
For some far other countryside
Than that grey Ireland he had known,
Yet on his dream of it was thrown
Some light from that consuming Fire
Which is the end of all desire.
If men adore It as the power
Empires and cities tower on tower
Are built in worship by the way
High Babylon or Nineveh.
Seek It as love and there may be
A Golden Age and Arcady.
All shadows are they of one thing
To which all life is journeying.

FROM
Vale and Other Poems

TO
Seumas O'Sullivan

Vale

This was the heavenly hiding-place
    Wherein the spirit laughed a day.
All its proud ivories and fires
    Shrunk to a shovelful of clay.

It must have love, this silent earth,
    To leap up at the King's desire,
Moving in such a noble dance
    Of wreathed ivory and fire.

It will not stir for me at all,
    Nor answer me with voice or gleam.
Adieu, sweet-memoried dust, I go
    After the Master for the dream.

The Gay

Those moon-gilded dancers
Prankt like butterflies,
Theirs was such lovely folly
It stayed my rapt eyes:
But my heart that was pondering
Was sadly wise.

To be so lighthearted
What pain was left behind;
What fetters fallen gave them
Unto this airy mind:
What dark sins were pardoned;
What God was kind!

I with long anguish bought
Joy that was soon in flight;
And wondered what these paid
For years of young delight;
Ere they were born what tears
Through what long night.

All these gay cheeks, light feet,
Were telling over again,
But in a heavenly accent,
A tale of ancient pain
That, the joy spent, must pass
To sorrow again.

The Gay

I went into the wilderness
Of night to be alone,
Holding sorrow and joy
Hugged to my heart as one,
Lest they fly on those wild ways
And life be undone.

Blight

They stilled the sweetest breath of song
Who loosed from love its chains,
Who made it easy to be borne,
A thing that had no pains.

A dusk has blighted Psyche's wings
And the wild beauty dies.
The fragrance and the glow were born
From its own agonies.

How?

How can Death ever make a tryst for me
With those whose long heart-hoarded images
Still look upon me with unfallen youth
Out of the happy isles of memory?
Passed from themselves and far from me, their light
Lost in an unimaginable Light
Or sunken to dark flame, I might not know
Nor soul nor body. But save Death restore
Those heaven-climbers I had known when young
Life has been vain. I am as one who takes
An angel-haunted road to find it fade
In a void desert. I must meet again
That slender-lovely candle of the Lord,
Wife of my friend, and unto all his friends
A gentle sister, and that handsome youth
From reverie that seemed like indolence
Waking with haughty transcendental speech
That whipt the will, and our grey visitor
Who taught me not in words, but gave to me,
In vision on the intellectual air,
The noble images that once were seen
In the ritual of the holy mysteries,
The unconsumable, unsubduable,
Winged, airy beauty of Psyche, born
From this thick husk, as in Hellenic myth
The glittering goddess from the head of Zeus
Uprose—all who were on the path with me,
Lamp-bearing pilgrims. But can Death appoint
A trysting-place where ancient shall be young,

The fallen upright, those on heavenly heights
Shrink to the stature that I knew them by?
And will they tryst with one who may to them
Be as a candle blown long, long ago?
I know not how our wandering lives may mix
In the hereafter, save that it may be true,
That ancient imagination of the seers
Of a profundity where all that was,
Or ever shall be, glows and breathes in an
Eternal present. Thither might I come
After the putrifying, when towards us
The majesty is melted, and becomes
Tender as to a child, and breathes in us,
And life is winged and wonderful and gay,
And we are ever hurrying to a Youth
Older than Time, though it bedrape itself
With phantoms of our youth that blossom ever
With loveliness of Uncreated Light.
If after the stern putrifying fires
Death brings us to a so transfigured past
Within the Everlasting, and we can take
From all that is whatever is our own,
Life has been justified. For if our dreams
Be not immortal, the soul is not. The soul
Is but a congregation of high dreams.

Enchantment

On this fawn-coloured shore
All delicately strewn,
Gold dust and gleaming shell,
White stone and blue stone,
Lie sweetly together whether
Eyes be to see them or none.

The air is gay with voices
Of children. The sun
Casts flowers of purple shadow
Before them as they run,
Blows clouds and blooms of shadow
Where the swift feet may run.

Onward the children race
To leap into the sea
That bubbles silver bright
In the lovely revelry
Of foam and limbs together
In a white revelry.

How grew that airy tumult
On shores that were so still,
That wind of flowers and shadows?
What art invisible
Made all that airy wonder,
At what enchanter's will?

Sibyl

A myriad loves
Her heart would confess,
That though but one
To be wantonness.

And this was why
She could not stay,
From the gilded fireside
Running away.

To be on the hillside,
Gay and alone
A twilight sibyl,
With rock for her throne.

There she was sweetheart
To magical things,
To cloudland, woodland,
Mountains and springs.

She yielded to them
But was not the less
Pure, but the more
For that wantonness.

For through these lovers
Her spirit grew
To be clear as crystal
And cool as dew.

Sibyl

Their bridal gift
Was to make her be
Initiate
Of their company;

To know the lovely
Voices of these,
Of light, of earth,
Of winds and of seas,

Whose wisdom flowed
From a fullness; yea,
From bygone ages
And far away.

So thronged was her spirit
It seemed a pack
That carried the moon
And stars on her back.

When the spirit wakens
It will not have less
Than the whole of life
For its tenderness.

And that was why
She could not stay,
From the gilded fireside
Running away.

She laughed in herself
On her seat of stone,
"It would be wanton
To love but one."

Will o' the Wisp

I, with remembrance of our childhood only,
Was stayed astonished at so vast a Youth,
That bloomed suddenly through grey stones and air,
Laughing, whirling, juggling its shining balls
In their azure goblets, playing at hide and seek,
An elf in the ivory delicate wild rose,
Dilated at the zenith, sparkling afar,
Here blurring the brown rough earth with beauty,
Dancing to a greybeard as to a child.
O thou Ancient with Youth, dost Thou see in me
The airy child who may so soon go forth?
Art Thou the companion who shall take my hand
In the dark valley? Wilt Thou wear again
The shapes that were Thy lovely hiding-places
Where I found Thee of old, secret in eyes,
Inviolate on lips and in the heart
Unconquerable? There was always for Thee
A door of escaping through which I could not follow.
Even now, tenderly frolic and intimate,
If I would stay Thee, at once invisible
Thou art gone inward, and Thy light as lost
As the flying fishes, a pearly flicker that leaps
From the dark blue to slide in the dark blue.
As the high Emperor I have never
Worshipped Thee, making my dreams majestical
With thrones girt by the warriors of heaven.
My secret was Thy gentleness. I know
No nurse had ever crooned a lullaby
So softly as Thou the music that guides the loud

Will o' the Wisp

Tempest in its going forth. I know full well
When Thou dancest into the heart that it may be
The rending of the heart. Yet the saints found,
Clinging unto Thee, that their anguish burned
Upward to unimaginable delight.
I had not passion to press so to Thee
To know Thee as the Might or the Wise.
But that I worshipped with so light a love
I was repaid, for every hour was heaped
With a new changing beauty that was still
The Ancient Beauty. Here it glows on me
Within Thy many-coloured garden, twilight,
A beauty that has never been before,
Save for one silvery bloom, the Evening Star.

"The Things Seen"

The shadow drifted apart leaving the shadowless soul;
A high, winged, glittering, airy creature of the sky.
What had we known of it but a fugitive flash of wing?
We had been drowned in our own shadows, you and I.

Our love was breathed upon phantom lips; shade wrought with shade.
Oh, beloved, it was not I, but the shadow, who cried
In bitterness, who stabbed. Oh, world, they were shadows too,
Who bound their gods to the cross, and those who were crucified.

Midsummer Eve

On this even the ways are clear,
Crystal to the wizard eye.
Every pathway to the seer
Winds on into infinity.
But in this enchanted hour
Look you gravely where you pass;
Fear to scar the delicate grass.
Such a titan tender power
Revives it from the summer heat,
It must be sacred to your feet.

On this night of many days
Rocks shall give to your amaze
They shall be hollow to your eyes,
Though now you may not tread the ways
Star-lit, god-guarded, leading to
The City of the Mysteries.

To the gentler thought that drew
Thee unto the oaken glade
Thou mayest yield. Its ebon shade,
Where the tattered moonlight reels
Dancing on pearly toes and heels
Shall break into a lovelier dance.
Dryad and Hamadryad there
Shall awaken from their trance,
Moving with the high, innocent air
And manner of lost Paradise

But would you a more daring will,
Toss dice betwixt the fool and wise?
The coracle is on the shore,
Yonder the shadowy heaving hill
Where music draws the heart to haste
Over that moon-coloured waste
Of crumbling foam. Above its roar
Far off the noble Sirens pour—
The choristers of Heavenly mind—
Their old misrepresented song,
The music that can work no wrong.
Even who come by it to death,
Whose souls through some green gloom pursue
The silver bubbles of the breath,
In that wide aether they come to,
The song they heard shall tune the ear
Unto the music of that sphere,
The shining of the mystic maid
Be a gold candle in its share.

Yet on this night have holy care.
All things put on their loveliest dress.
The fallen angels of the heart
Their ancient, angel faces wear,
A heart-consuming tenderness,
Though it may be a wanton thing
Walks like a Daughter of the King.
Hardly the saint may with much prayer
Make his soul meet for Paradise,
Who met nor knew in their disguise
The sultry Children of the Air,
And from the tempting of their eyes
Built up a heaven for the red dust

Midsummer Eve

Out of a light-transfiguring lust.
If the deep night assail thee so
With unappeasable desires,
Fly from thy solitude and go
Where the gay children light their fires,
And whirl in air the blazing whin,
And shake fire crystals through the gloom,
Nor know what hosts have gathered in
To walk with them the ancient room.
Their hardy innocence knows naught
Of the wild peril of thy thought,
That brought thee to this tragic place
Where good and evil have one face.
And only the true seer can find
The bright star, or the dark, behind
The mask of beauty that all wear.

Fear lest thy dream melt in desire
And it should wear a face so sweet
You may not know of what dark fire
Is hidden in the lovely cheat.
Yet be not coward through much care.
What shall they have, the wise who stay
By the familiar ways, whose heart
Still clings to altar, field or mart,
Who deem that prudence to be wise,
Who shun the infinite desire,
And never make the sacrifice
By which the soul is changed to fire?
These prudent when they come to die
And their road breaks in sudden sky,
They shall be blind and lonely there,
Nor know of its high Emperor.

Those only see where spirits are
A glory, a self-shining star.
All roads are safe to thee this night
If thou dost walk by thine own light.

Retribution

The soul into itself withdraws, thinking on all
The gay, heroical ardours it forsook; the years
That were made over-sweet with passion; the tears
Love wept, dying of its own fullness; and the fall
Into the pit where seven unholy spirits conspire
Against the Holy Ones, turning the sky-born fire
Unto infernal uses, feeding beauty to the beast.
Remembering the dark joys that were born of the feast,
It dreads the everlasting fire, the torment of sense.
Oh, unhappy, the judge is not without thee but within,
Who shall condemn thee, as retribution for they sin,
To the consuming fire of thine own penitence.

Ancestry

Had thine art not skill to change
Dream into a deed of sense?
Did the baffled heart recoil
On itself in penitence?

When thy lovely sin has been
Wasted in a long despair,
World-forgetting, it may look
Upon thee with an angel air.

There was never sin of thine
But within its heart did dwell
A beauty that could whisper thee
Of the high heaven from which it fell.

Germinal

Call not thy wanderer home as yet
    Though it be late.
Now is his first assailing of
    The invisible gate.
Be still through that light knocking. The hour
    Is thronged with fate.

To that first tapping at the invisible door
    Fate answereth.
What shining image or voice, what sigh
    Or honied breath,
Comes forth, shall be the master of life
    Even to death.

Satyrs may follow after. Seraphs
    On crystal wing
May blaze. But the delicate first comer
    It shall be King.
They shall obey, even the mightiest,
    That gentle thing.

All the strong powers of Dante were bowed
    To a child's mild eyes,
That wrought within him that travail
    From depths up to skies,
Inferno, Purgatorio
    And Paradise.

Amid the soul's grave councillors
    A petulant boy
Laughs under the laurels and purples, the elf
    Who snatched at his joy,
Ordering Caesar's legions to bring him
    The world for his toy.

In ancient shadows and twilights
    Where childhood had strayed,
The world's great sorrows were born
    And its heroes were made.
In the lost boyhood of Judas
    Christ was betrayed.

Let thy young wanderer dream on:
    Call him not home.
A door opens, a breath, a voice
    From the ancient room,
Speaks to him now. Be it dark or bright
    He is knit with his doom.

Companions

We have a choice when young
Of an immortal friend,
One of the shining host,
Who will come to us at our call
And stay with us to the end.

When I was in my youth
I called the starry Child
To play with me in my thought
Who breathed sweetness and joy,
Making lovely the wild.

Now body and soul stumble
And heart is filled with ruth;
Yet the other lightly moves
Breathing within a ruin
The bitter fragrance of youth.

Oh, had my youth been wise
I had called upon the Sage—
Not on that starry Child.
What had been harsh to youth
Would have been sweet in age.

Too burning bright, that Child
Drawn from the heavenly air,
By the magic will of youth—
Our prayers are always answered.
Oh, to be wise in prayer!

Tirnanoge

A Dream

We were happy and dead, you and I.
    With the gay light footfall of dream
We followed the moon through the hills
    By a quivering jewel of stream.

We were happy and dead, you and I.
    For all things ran at our will.
The genii of earth and of sky,
    Blue night, and moon-coloured rill,

And the mountains crouched by our side,
    Were a pulse of the spirit more gay,
Would arise and shine with delight
    In the gold and the silver of day.

In the valleys Death gave us for joy
    There were voices and lights that we knew,
Earth's fables of love and of beauty
    That Death had brought to be true.

Forgetfulness

The hills have vanished in dark air;
And night, without an eye, is blind.
I too am starless. Time has blurred
The aeons of my life behind.

Oh, what in those dark aeons lay?
What tumult, beauty and desire?
I know not, all are lost beyond
Sunsets of anguish and of fire.

Earth-Bound

Soul whirl with young body
    In a frolic so gay
It grew forgetful of
    Its heavenly yesterday,
Its natural solemn music,
    So giddy was the play,

Then body grew a-weary
    And leaned to soul in tears;
But soul was dreaming over
    The folly of young years.
It had nothing but ancient folly
    To soothe its lover's fears.

When body lay in stillness
    The soul could not recall
The airy solemn being
    It had before its fall.
It was tangled in old folly:
    The earth had it in thrall.

The Cities

They shall sink under water,
They shall rise up again:
They shall be peopled
By millions of men.

Cleansed of their scarlet,
Absolved of their sin,
They shall be like crystal
All stainless within.

Paris and Babel,
London and Tyre,
Reborn from the darkness,
Shall sparkle like fire.

From the folk who throng in
Their gardens and towers
Shall be blown fragrance
Sweeter than flowers.

Faery shall dance in
The streets of the town,
And from sky headlands
The gods looking down.

Atlantic

How lonely and lovely those valleys
    That quivered with silver and gold,
And changed in a dream to blue mountains
    From which snow was uprolled.

How white was the sun in the heaven,
    And over the glitter of snow
That fell from those hills to those hollows
    Seven Fires were aglow.

For what winged and wonderful creatures
    Shall this wide beauty be home?
Their feet who would tread on these meadows
    Must be lighter than foam.

When earth is outworn for the spirit,
    Its body made light by desire,
Shall it walk on this glory of waters
    Ere it climb through the air to the Fire.

The Farewell of Pan

This might be Pan's last supper for me, so solemn the house;
His sweet apostles bend so tenderly their brows:
They spread the table with stars and scents, and with me share
The odorous bread of earth, the holy wine of air.
Lest I remember scarlet hours they make all new,
Hang the dusk tapestries and spray with coolth of dew.
They cleanse the feet that danced at the satyric sport
With fauns and silvery witches at the Midnight Court
And I forget the goat heels and the shaggy thighs
For the face so lofty, the voice so gentle, and the eyes so wise.
"Farewell, farewell, O fortunate for whom death waits;
O bird who shall be winged when the body opens its gates:
Who can fly to the Infinite Glory. We, who are slaves of its law,
Who harden the pure to diamond and break the base like a straw;
Exiled, we pine for the King in His beauty. We long for the day
When this shadow show shall be over, the masks we wore thrown away—
The monstrous masks that veiled us, of satyr, demon and faun—
And be lovely, starry and ancient with you as we were in the dawn.
Be swift, O winged one, be swift to the King, and tell
Our anguish exiled from His beauty. Fly swift, free bird, and farewell!"

FROM
The House of the Titans

TO
Osborn Bergin

Earth Spirit

O dark holy magic,
To steal out at dawn,
To dip face and feet in grasses
The few trembles on,
Ere its might be spirit healing
Be broken by the dawn.

O to reel drunken
On the heady dew.
To know again the virgin wonder
That boyhood knew,
While words run to music, giving voices
To the voiceless dew.

They will make, those dawn-wandering
Lights and airs,
The bowed worshipping spirit
To shine like theirs,
They will give to thy lips an aeolian
Music like theirs.

Comfort

The skies were dim and vast and deep
Above the vale of rest.
They seemed to rock the stars to sleep
Beyond the mountain's crest.

I sought for graves I mourned, but found
The roads were blind. The grave,
Even of love, heart-lost, was drowned
Under time's brimming wave.

Huddled beneath the wheeling sky,
Strange was my comfort there:
That stars and stones and love and I
Drew to one sepulchre.

Lost Talisman

Those images of beauty
That once I did despise,
Now in my age I cherish
And clutch with miser's eyes.
Even for one frail blossom
I will make sacrifice.

Once there were other treasures
I had, O strange to say,
Made dim those magic blossoms
And I cast them away.
I cast beauty from me
As a god child might in play.

O what was in the being
Of boyhood that could make
Beauty seem but a glimmer
That followed in the wake
Of some proud sails set sunward
On some enchanted lake?

Two Magics

Have they the same enchantment, these children straying
In streets where electric moonlight and scintillating rose
Shed blooms on the ashen air, as those other children
Crouched in trance under hedgerows where hawthorn
    thickens its snows;

Or those others, who under a real moon and stars
Move to deeper wonder in themselves, who are still,
Who touch each other but gently, lest they break the magic
That makes them one with it on the night-shadowy hill.

Incarnation

Thou slender of limb; thou lightness;
Wild grace that flies
Over the shining sand
Under cloud-brilliant skies:
What beauty flies within thee,
Sped from what skies?

Thee for an instant
The god possesses,
Is joy in thy fleet limbs,
Gay feet and flying tresses.
His lovely thought of thee the artist
Delights in the caresses.

Thou shalt remember hereafter
Through sorrowful years
That wonder of all thy moments,
And pine for through tears
This moment that shall be for thee
A fountain of tears.

Karma

All that was harsh or sweet
To me was brought
Through some affinity
With soul or sense or thought.
I complain not nor wonder.
Just was my lot.

I ask the wise to say
Why are we heir
To the wonder of the sky,
The shining there.
What justice gave me
This star-enchanted air?

Is there still in us
A heaven-descended ray
Of that which built the palaces
Of night and day?
Do our first works, sun, moon, and stars,
Shine on our clay?

O, how my heart leaps up!
It can laugh. It could fly,
Even in dream being knit
To that majesty!
Though long passed from our glory,
I can sing! I could fly!

What Home

O, how I wreaked my childhood's spite
When I first dwindled to this day,
Thinking on my lost wonder world
That was so very far away.

And now my heart has come to rest,
Or the green earth has homelier grown.
Its children creep into my heart,
Woodland and water, hill and stone.

When I return to walk amid
The thrones of light, O shall I dream
Of the lost earth, a cloudy hill,
A shadowy vale, a flickering stream!

A Mountain Tarn

The pool glowed to a magic cauldron
O'er which I bent alone.
The sun burned fiercely on the waters,
The setting sun:
A madness of fire: around it
A dark glory of stone.

O mystic fire!
Stillness of earth and air!
That burning silence I
For an instant share.
In the crystal of quiet I gaze
And the god is there.

Within that loneliness
What multitude!
In the silence what ancient promise
Again renewed!
Then the wonder goes from the stones,
The lake and the shadowy wood.

The Dark Lady

O, no, I was not wanton with that man.
But to his imaginations, yes. I made
Myself a hundred natures. It is writ,
My myriad girlhood, in that printed page.
Or was it I? Did I but play the part
His magic plotted for me? Did he know
That his imaginations lived in me
And swayed me to be one of their own kind,
To act the bawd for whom an emperor
Might cast his world away: or it might be
A maid to whom the world had never come,
All-innocent upon a fairy isle?
Yet at the court of the great queen I had
But one disdainful face, however many
Wild hearts might beat within me: and high lords
And admirals, who had wrecked Armadas, were
Wrecked on a flinty look. O, I remember.
My heart swoons to think upon that hour,
When a young learnèd gentleman, his head
Dizzy with gaudy words that had caught fire
From sun and moon, importuned me to know
The latest prince of speech. And I was swept,
Half laughing and half scornful, to my fate.
Yet I had not been one hour in the room
Ere I was lit by many torches, and
Knew, being in that humble lodging-house,
That I had come unto a lordlier court
Than the great queen's, a court where kings
    and princes

Robeless could awe by their own majesty,
Or, being bare to the spirit, seemed as low
As if they had not legions at their call.
And there were elves that frolicked in his thought,
And giddy knaves whose very sins seemed rooted
In a wild nature, and might win them heaven
To make laughter for angels. I knew a man
Who held these very knaves had much to teach us
As the apostles: and we would lose less
Missing the queen of the dawn out of the myths,
Juno, with grave eyes under heavenly brows
And proud, starred peacocks, than if his rascal Jack
Had never lived in story. Not at once
Did I know all. No man will ever know
The mystery of his being, of multitudes
Within one spirit. Yet I knew from the first
That they were with him, incorporeal real,
Taking immortal bodies from sweet sounds,
Leaping into our thought as the gay moon,
A slippery dancer, reels from wave to wave.
He had hardly spoken ere a spirit of his
Had flashed within me, and I had made answer
Out of its nature. He turned upon me eyes
So wonder-wise, so humorous-kind, that I
Was melted from my art of dignity
And became once more the laughing girl who ran
Under her father's elms, who knew no rank
But life; jesting with folly; with her wit
Pelting both lords and grooms. O, the sweet play,
When all the delicate spirit's aflame, and point
With its own fire and airy rapier, nor knows
In that obscurity of delight the end
That it desires, the point in the other's breast.
For we are both half fearing and half faining

The Dark Lady

The exquisite anguish of our piercèd heart.
So flashed our speech. The first of many times.
I had not more easily as a small child
Told my heart stories than I could to him
Tell everything in thought, as if he were
An ampler, wider heart-nurse to myself.
And though I was all love I shrank from that,
The mating of lips and body, lest having all
I should have less than love; in the king's bed
Be absent from his court. And when I was
Within myself, the angels of wisdom and love
Held passionate council in me. I was rent
By images of love and by their martyrdoms,
For I had buried many an image deep
In the heart's doubt what would be noble to do.
And for there was that warfare in me the girl
Was ripened to full woman. I looked back
Upon the woman I had been before
As she upon her childhood. I was, I think,
The only creature that by flesh and blood
Entered the court of his spirit: and all others
Came through some crystal mystic gate unto
The throne of his heart as vassals might, and left
Not tribute of pearl, ivory or gold
But breathed their very spirits into him
That he would dress as emperors and clowns,
Play one against another. I do believe
The mighty dead from unimagined homes
Dreamed back their greatness and their frailty,
The very lion-front that awed the world,
Shaking it by the thunder of words that fell
From the imperious heaven of the high will.
And how could it be other? We are not gods
To create life, and only what is given us

Order and rule. I know it, I, that was
A glowing mirror to him, would sometimes,
Ere he had spoken, find living in myself
His latest imagination, the very trick
Of its mood, and hear it afterwards
Dressed in the actor's body cry on a stage.
If it was so with me, might he not be
A hostel for all life? For some design,
I know not what. Perhaps that we who play
Upon our surfaces might pry more deep
In our rich mystery, the way be pointed
That life must travel. I thought it so, that he
Was magicked by the gods for their design,
And I was handmaid to it. O how frail
The instruments the gods must use in us!
There came to the queen's court their masterpiece,
A boy that stayed the breath, all glow and fire,
Unflawed, so airy ivory of limb
He might have leaped from an archangel's dream.
And was it destiny that two such wonders
Of soul and body should meet, be to each other
Mystery and enchantment: beauty that had
No soul but beauty itself: and the wise soul,
Baffled in reading where there was not mind,
Fell into dreaming, and at last was stayed
On the body's miracle. And I grew sick
Seeing the dawn of an unnatural love,
The kind that marred the Grecian genius,
    and closed
The nobleness of mind that had begun
With Homer's tale. I cried upon myself
As all corrupt to so misread the eyes
That rested on the boy, or the sweet words.
But when I knew that I had not misread,

The Dark Lady

O, what heart-shaking, what deep fountains
   of scorn
Or pity broke out like madness. I lay awake
Buffeted by fierce winds from heaven and hell,
Searching the blackness of my night for God.
And knew not whether God or devil counselled,
Self-love, or love that crucifies itself,
Or anguished of long-stemmed desire to have
What passes from it. But I thought to stay
That love unnatural lest his spirit's walls
Should thicken, and there be a solitude
In that high court. And I used every art
Of heart and body and gave the body to him,
And had no joy in giving. The holy fires
Whereof the Elohim compounded us
If they glow not to one pure breathing, but
Are all disordered, war in us and burn us
By hurt of beauty or love, or wisdom cries,
A mourner in the thick of erring delight.
And he to whom I was no mystery,
But a dear friend, stayed not his heart on me,
For that infinitude of his wide mind,
Searching ever for the undiscovered heart,
Wandered away from me unto that one
Beautiful, baleful and uncharted star
Of boyhood. I knew my sacrifice was vain
And a new madness shook me, making me
All pitiless, with a mad woman's will
To win her way even if soul be lost.
And all affections in me, made bitter, changed
In dark reverse unto their opposites.
I was as one who hears an angel sing
To a sweet lute, then turns to her dark angel
To sing the same song to the trembling strings,

And pure and holy are made poisonous.
When we are maddened, and the goblins in us
Riot in incredible loves and hates,
I do not know if god or demon guides
The storm while we are blinded. I was not
The same although I moved to the same end.
For now I was all hopeless in love, yet played
With all my woman's art upon the boy,
Meeting him in palace chambers or
In garden alleys. I was I know not what
Unconquered and rich wonder to his youth
That had won all easily before, but now
Met but a lovely mockery when he prayed;
And the unravished beauty was to him,
As with that other, the sole star of the heart.
And so I drew him, half forgetting at times
My purpose and some wildness in my blood
Conspired together. I yielded to him, became
A lover unto two, one godlike in mind
And one, the outer image of a god.
And in intoxication of conquest the boy
Wore all a victor's airs with me until
Even rumour had no further secrets to tell.
And then at last one day I met the other
And he had known, and never was there face
So ravaged, and my heart in every beat
Let rain a drop all fiery red. There was
I know not what wild pity in my eyes,
And the god knows that at no other time
Was I so lost from myself, so terribly his.
Yet at his anguished words I wore the air
Of one bred in the gay court of the world
Above the ceremony by which the herd
Order their ways, one who took carelessly

The Dark Lady

This love or that, and knew no obligation
But to win fuel to keep high one's fire.
He could not read me, my heart-aching
 humour—
For I was not then in his heart that never
Misread, but only an apparition to his eyes—
When I likened myself to him, the myriad-
 minded
Who gathered knaves and heroes with like love
To snatch the inmost secret of them, so I,
Seeking as rich a wisdom, must, being woman,
Who win only by the body, search the soul
At its full tide in the completeness of love,
When, to the vigilant spirit, it is quick
With all it is. And I had not yet won
Spirits enough to be a mate for him
Learned in so many hearts. He threw at me
A single word. I, who had masked my soul
As the proud queen of harlots to deceive,
Was yet angered he should be credulous,
And all that was still virginal in me,
And all my passion he should be deceived,
Cried furiously in bitter and wild speech
That spurned him. When god and devil through
 one voice
Cry the same words they scorch when double fire.
And he, the mighty seer, looked for a moment
Upon me as if spirit and sense in him
Were sundered. With no other word he went.
He saw me never again. Yet I was victor
Slaying the unnatural with the natural love.
And I do think for all my bruisèd heart
I was more happy than he. I can but guess
From that he made the bitter Troilus speak

Of Cressid in how many blazing fires
His anger burned me. Still I dreamed of that
Rich court so many coloured once. But now,
O, what dark travellers scoured to that dark house
Brought as unto the nether sovereignty
Tribute of raving madness, guilt and fear,
Unto that one whose fearful artistry
With pigments of midnight, eclipse and fire
Could make them visible for ever. And yet
I think that I, who had vanished from his eyes,
Was still within him. For he, who painted me
In many scarlet dyes, came ere the end
To breathe forgiveness. I had once imagined
For his delight myself to be a maid
Bred on a fairy isle who knew not man,
And I played for him with what innocence
The maid would greet a lover who came to her.
And at the last he had fondled in his thought
My tender fantasy, and made himself
An enchanter with spirits at his command
And they had loved each other. So I think
That he had come to know himself and me.
O, why are we not certain about our deeds!
There was another dread enchanter imagined
A circle in the kingdom of the dead,
Where sinful lovers, who are blown about
In an eternal storm, cling to each other.
I thought that I, even on that stormy air,
Would have eternal joy were I the one
To whom his hands clung in the eternal shade.
And brooding on that poet's tale I dreamt
That I was so blown about with one
Who held to me, but when I saw his face
It was not the face I loved, but was the face

The Dark Lady

Beautiful, mad, hopeless, of that boy.
And I awoke. I had been weeping in sleep
And all my pillow was a wetness of tears.

Dana

I am the tender voice calling "Away,"
Whispering between the beatings of the heart,
And inaccessible in dewy eyes
I dwell, and all unkissed on lovely lips,
Lingering between white breasts inviolate,
And fleeting ever from the passionate touch,
I shine afar, till men may not divine
Whether it is the stars or the beloved
They follow with rapt spirit. And I weave
My spells at evening, folding with dim caress,
Aerial arms and twilight dropping hair,
The lonely wanderer by wood or shore,
Till, filled with some deep tenderness, he yields,
Feeling in dreams for the dear mother heart
He knew, ere he forsook the starry way,
And clings there, pillowed far above the smoke
And the dim murmur from the duns of men.
I can enchant the trees and rocks, and fill
The dumb brown lips of earth with mystery,
Make them reveal or hide the god. I breathe
A deeper pity than all love, myself
Mother of all, but without hands to heal:
Too vast and vague, they know me not. But yet,
I am the heartbreak over fallen things,
The sudden gentleness that stays the blow,
And I am in the kiss that foemen give
Pausing in battle, and in the tears that fall
Over the vanquished foe, and in the highest,
Among the Danaan gods, I am the last

Dana

Council of mercy in their hearts where they
Mete justice from a thousand starry thrones.
My heart shall be in thine when thine forgives.

The Warrior of Heaven

Though I have might to roll the stars through air,
And all the gods are suppliant of my power,
And what they do is portion of my strength,
I was made master by the All-Father only
Because I was the gentlest of the gods.
And, though I make fierce war upon the anarchs,
My myrmidons are frail and delicate things.
I hide within a blossom and its still beauty
Becomes might as a star and none may touch it.
I can stay the march of armies by a child.
When I look through its eyes and passionate hand
Falls, and the soul in awful penitence
Hides in itself. And with a twilight air
I can make anchorites of kings. I overcome
Fierce things by gentleness. And my allies
Against the thunder of congregated powers
Are silences in heaven, the light in valleys,
The smoke above the roof, the quiet hearth,
The well-beloved things that come to be
Images of peace in the All-Father's being.
No sentinel can stay them, and they make
Traitors to glory and pride. And so I gather
Invincible armies that can invade
The secret places of the spirit, until
Even the comets and mad meteors,
The lions of the wilderness of space,
Who roam with fiery manes, the potentates
Of air and earth, rulers of thrones and powers,
Melted within themselves give fealty,

The Warrior of Heaven

And build together till the dream of life
Mirrors the All-Father's being, and that
Can know itself in us as we in him.
When thou art of thine own will defenceless
As the fragile flickering moth or trembling grass,
I shall be champion for thee. Thou shalt find
Invisible legions breathing love for thee
Through the dark clay, or from the murmuring air,
And by the margin of the deep. And when
Thy spirit becomes so gentle it could pass
Into another spirit and leave no wound,
I will give unto thee this star to lead.

A Farewell

I look on wood and hill and sky,
    Yet without any tears
To the warm earth I bid good-bye
    For what unnumbered years.

So many times my spirit went
    This dark transfiguring way,
Nor ever knew what dying meant,
    Deep night or a new day.

So many times it went and came,
    Deeper than thought it knows
Unto what majesty of flame
    In what wide heaven it goes.

An Evening with A.E.

I was lonely in Dublin. A.E.—George Russell—was gone.

In the summer of 1935 death came to "The Bearded Plato", and Dublin is not the same. The familiar figure that had so often strode the streets of the capital of the Free State with a kind of Olympian grandeur would cross Merrion Square no more. One of Ireland's greatest sons had gone to join John M. Synge, Clarence Mangan, Sir Richard Steele, Edmund Burke, Oliver Goldsmith, and others of the immortal company. I strolled over St. Stephen's Green in the mystic twilight, oblivious to the lovers sitting on the benches and pretending to be watching the swans on the lake. I did not hear their soft-spoken speech nor observe their bold caresses. I was living over again the magic evening I spent with A.E. in Dublin in the summer of 1923.

I.

I had come to war-scourged, politically-crazed southern Ireland that summer fourteen years before, to write a series of articles on the sorry conditions caused by the disastrous division among the Sinn Féiners. I carried letters to the leaders of both factions, as well as to several celebrities. But I had no letter to A.E., and I speculated as to how I might manage to meet him. The resourceful doorman, so long a picturesque fixture at the Shelbourne Hotel, proved to be as effective as the best letter of introduction signed by a somebody. "Nothing would be easier," he explained, "Mr. Russell passes here every day. I'll hail him and tell him there's an American gentleman here who wants to meet him." It sounded easy, too easy, I thought. But the next day, just after breakfast, the doorman called to me: "Here's Mr. Russell," he announced. And so it was. A.E. himself, broad-shouldered, stoutly framed, bronze beard, his fine eyes twinkling, his friendly hand extended. I took it eagerly. A.E. was pulling at a pipe and trailing clouds of smoke. He took the pipe from his bearded lips. "What can I do for you?" he said.

"Could you give me an hour of your time?" I ventured.

"Certainly, and more than an hour if you wish it. Can't you come to my home? Would tomorrow evening suit your convenience?"

I think I gasped as I answered, "It would."

As I waited to keep my appointment with Mr. Russell I learned the origin of his arresting pen name. The story goes that he was in the National Library in Dublin waiting for the attendant to give him a book, when his eye fell on a dictionary of religion that was lying open on a table. The first word that caught his eye was "Aeon", and it was explained as "a word by Gnostics to designate the first created beings." Young Russell was impressed, and so great was the impression that he has ever since called himself by the first two letters of the word "Aeon". He intended to take "Aeon" as a pseudonym, but a printer, no finding his handwriting easy to decipher, printed only the first two letters and added a question mark. Russell in his proof deleted the question mark and left "A.E." standing. Such is the history of the cryptic letters by which one of the most famous Dubliners of his day was known the world around.

An Evening with A.E.

II.

One seldom sees a personage at his best save in his own castle among his books, pictures and other treasures, and thus it was I saw A.E.

His house was unpretentious, quite modest in fact, but comfortable and homey. The room in which he received me was part library, part studio, a "den" worthy the name. His books—the volumes he handled and knew as a man knows his wife and children—possibly better—were there. And the pictures—his own handiwork—varied and lovely scenes of Irish lands, mountains and waters, vivid in colouring and of a brooding, mystic beauty; a few portraits of Irish contemporary celebrities, his friends—such were the appointments of the room where we talked that golden evening through.

Candidly, I do not regard a beard as an asset to "manly beauty"; rather the contrary, in fact. But I am willing to make an exception in the case of A.E., the "bearded Plato". There was something in his appearance that suggested the portraits of Roscoe Conkling, only the imperiousness and arrogant air of the eminent American senator were wholly absent, and in their place a modest, elegant gentleman of Chesterfieldian graces. A.E.'s longish brown pointed beard was showing a little grey; his head crowned with Tennysonian locks was massive and noble. I see him now—the flowing windsor tie, grey tweed lounge suit, loose and comfortable, mark the ease and fluency of the man, feel the warmth of his radiant personality, calm, poised, yet buoyant, the whole man very much alive. A.E. lived up to his reputation fully, a thing that cannot be said of all celebrities.

Pipe in hand oftener than between his teeth, he talked literature, not merely about it, and discussed politics with a sanity and breadth of view not common in Ireland at that day. The man was a mystic, yet his feet were firmly planted on the earth. He commented freely on numerous subjects, and gave his estimate of the personalities then looming in Ireland. As I listened to his appraisal of men, books and events, a phrase of Lowell's in his famous "Commemoration Ode" flashed through my mind. Here indeed is one of "Plutarch's men", I thought.

III.

"Ireland, I fear, is no longer an island of saints, unless it be plaster saints." A.E.'s brown eyes smiled at me through wreaths of smoke as he pulled at his pipe. "Idealism has suffered, but it is not wholly dead. It cannot wholly die in Ireland."

"What do you think of the long struggle for an Irish republic?"

"Some of my dearest friends are numbering among the Republicans." A.E.'s expressive eyes became tender, and he paused. "There was Erskine Childers"—he indicated a portrait on a nearby easel, his own portrait of Childers, and went on—"He was my friend, brilliant of mind, generous and beautiful of spirit. I think he was wrong in some of his political views, but what is more important, he was true to his convictions. Now, politics is not an exact science like mathematics, though some appear to think otherwise. Take such words as 'republic', 'nation', 'democracy'—these words are not transparent as some seem to believe, rather they are opaque words. A republican form of government by any other name would serve as well. A mere term is not worth dying for, a mere theory does not warrant a martyrdom as I see it. But there have been heroic souls who saw it differently, who died for a term, a word, a definition."

There was one question that had been on the tip of my tongue all evening. Two nights previous I had attended a mass meeting of Republicans at the Mansion House. The

An Evening with A.E.

place was crowded to overflowing and the enthusiasm perfervid. The day following, the press of Dublin all but ignored the Mansion House meeting though columns were devoted to the Free State campaign. I asked A.E. how he accounted for such discrimination on the part of the newspapers.

"The Republicans have nothing to say," he explained. "The people are tired of hearing the same thing over and over again. The Republicans need to restate their position and they could profit if they scrutinised carefully what is going on in Italy and Russia and other sections of society. The very least that they could do is to put their old wine in new bottles."

It was a clever answer, and his diagnosis of the Republican case may have been correct. Yet it did not wholly explain the attitude of Ireland's influential newspapers toward the "irregulars". For once I thought my Plato nodded.

IV.

A lengthy pause. A.E. stroked the long brown beard and puffed at his pipe thoughtfully. "The greatest men of Ireland who will be remembered longest were not the most brilliant, possibly," he mused. "We have had some towering leaders who, when they died, left nothing more substantial than the memory of a name—not to be belittled, I grant—yet not the noblest legacy, after all. Let me be specific. When the historian writes the story of modern Ireland he will, I think, chronicle the names of four men, two still living, whose monuments are observable in the nation's life. One of these will be Michael Davitt, who broke the back of feudalism in Ireland and started a movement which has made every tenant a potential proprietor of the soil he cultivates; another is Sir Horace Plunkett, who transformed the individualistic Ireland into a cooperative community, the end of which is not yet; a third is Dr. Douglas Hyde who pioneered fruitfully for the Gaelic revival and lives to see the achievement of much he fought for. The fourth is, I think, the one figure of heroic pattern out of a number who helped to bring in the democracy with which we are now experimenting—I refer to Arthur Griffith."

"Who is your favourite American writers?"

"Ah, Whitman, I should say. There was a man. I read him often. I like Emerson, too, your serenest soul. Recently I have been reading the poems of Edwin Arlington Robinson, and I find them stimulating. Then, I like what I have read of your man, Vachel Lindsay. You have an interesting country, young, virile, daring!"

A.E. dwelt much on the Gaelic revival, the labours of Douglas Hyde, Lady Gregory, W.B. Yeats and others. He was interested in the agrarian movement, having been associated with Sir Horace Plunkett in farming experiences, sketched the rise of Labour. Nothing human failed to engage his mind. He knew his Ireland, her strength and weakness, and he condemned lawlessness and disorder in emphatic terms. He did not, at that time, think highly of de Valera (he pronounced the name with the accent on the second syllable). Whether he came to think better of "Dev", I cannot say. Yet withal he was so gentle, so considerate and charitable in his estimate of men.

A.E. spoke of James Larkin, the Labour leader, now a member of the Free State parliament, a huge-framed man with a handsome Irish face. "The man has individuality and personal magnetism," he observed. "I was once on a tram when Larkin came in. Scarcely any of the passengers knew him by name, but as he came in and took a seat, we felt his presence.

V.

The topic switched to "dear, dirty Dublin". A.E.'s knowledge of the Free State capital was vast. He discoursed on

An Evening with A.E.

historic buildings, old houses, antiques, famed Dubliners, and inquired if I was familiar with a little book entitled *The Glamour of Dublin*, by D.L. Kelleher. When I told him I had never heard of the book, he arose, took down a slender volume from his shelves, explained that the chapters were brief, impressionistic and exquisitely phrased. "Listen to this," he said, and he read this paragraph from "Swift and Stella":

Such a night with clouds falling from the stars like hair unbound, and a lamenting wind moping and wandering over the city till even he shudders in that lamplit room, poring strangely over his papers, noting down and stopping with a start to drop his pen and strike with his palms upon the table and recover from an agony and so write again. Here in his dean's house, now fallen to be police station, is Swift the satirist. Swift the vitriol-tongue who can burn a parliament away with a phrase, Swift whose fame all envy but whose self there is none more to love. For over there by those torches and tapers they are laying her deep tonight in the Cathedral corner, out of his reach entirely now who has tortured her with riddles too long. No music at the end nor sunlight streaming through a painted window, no plumes but the smoke-wreaths of the pine, no tender organ notes to dim the dry coughing of the older clergy, and the "clatch, clatch" of shovels struck into the clay. So lay her down and leave her to the pitying dark, poor Stella who has been beguiled and baffled and wrecked by this intellect and enigma of the awful Swift. And for him as he drops his head upon his crossed palms while the lamp gutters out on the deanery room a little pity too! For, colossus of his day, yet does malign Fate stride him down with a fearful physical ill. And from his gloom and his secret hide, ye kind stars! and pass quickly telling it not to his neighbours, thou lamenting wind!

"Read some more," I pleaded. And in his rich, resonant voice he read the chapter on "The Phoenix Park Murder", when on "a lovely evening full of May-music of birds", Lord Frederick Cavendish and Under-Secretary Burke were foully slain by certain "clay-faced men". And he followed this with the mournful fragment devoted to "Wolfe Tone and his Martyrdom".

VI.

It was near midnight when I said I must go. A.E. took his hat, relit his pipe, and accompanied me two blocks, where I was to take a tram. The tram was late, so we continued to stroll. He was in a reminiscent mood, much to my delight, and I listened enraptured to his talk of men, of poetry, art, and religion. A moon half hidden by the misty night shone faintly overhead. There was the perfume of flowers on the night breeze. From the not far distant sea came the muffled blast of a ship's siren. I wished I might walk with this man for miles and miles. But the tram came all too soon.

Two days later I came away from Plunkett House with a copy of *The Interpreters* in my hands, and as I turned into St. Stephen's Green, I dropped down on a convenient bench and opened the volume. On the flyleaf was written: "George W. Russell, 'A.E.' " and under the signature these lines from one of his poems:

The few we are shall still unite
In fealty to unseen Kings
And unimaginable light.

An Evening with A.E.

The last time I saw A.E. was in Detroit in the winter of 1930, where he appeared in a lecture course at the Detroit Athletic Club. I was at the club to greet him when he arrived. He looked much older, the bronze beard was silvered, the great shoulders stooped a little, and I thought he was heavier than when I last saw him. He was tired, but his eyes were bright, and his voice as gentle and restful as ever. I accompanied him to his room and visited him there. Seated in an easy chair, his pipe going, he seemed to shed a dozen years. We talked of the religion of the mystics, and he cited to me St. Paul's reference to being caught up into the third heaven. "St. Paul was a mystic," he remarked. "There are many heavens, you know, at least seven, and how many more nobody knows." Then he spoke of the unity of the universe, the beauty that bathes the earth in celestial glory, the grandeur of the humblest life. I heard his lecture on Irish writers that evening, a discriminating and revealing hour. At its close I clasped his hand and looked into his eyes for the last time.

VII.

The same tall, gallant doorman is still at the Shelbourne; St. Stephen's Green is as lovely as of yesteryear; the green, white and orange flag of the Free State flutters proudly from Government House, where grave Eamon de Valera of the deeply lined face, one-time rebel, sits in the president's chair; the statues of Burke and Goldsmith keep their long vigil in front of Trinity College; the murky Liffey flows on toward the sea; but the bearded Plato holds court no more in Dublintown.

He speaks to us still in these lovely lines:

Selected Poems

When the trees and skies and fields are one in dusky wood,
Every heart of man is rapt within the mother's breast,
Full of peace and sleep and dreams in the vasty quietude
I am one with their hearts and at rest.

Edgar DeWitt Jones
20 April 1938

Poet, Seer and Scribe

> . . . *he took our wars into the palm of his thought*
> *and stroked the poisons from where we had fought.*
>
> – Thomas McCarthy, "The Wisdom of A.E."

Many of those who are familiar with George William Russell, better-known perhaps by his pseudonym A.E., will probably have come across him under the capacious shadow of his famous contemporary, William Butler Yeats. Russell was born in Lurgan, Co. Armagh on 10 April 1867 and moved to Dublin with his family when he was thirteen years old. The two poets met at art school in Dublin as young men in the 1880s and maintained a lifelong friendship, although they did not always see eye to eye, especially when Yeats's single-mindedness about the running of the Abbey Theatre offended the more collegial A.E. Despite this falling out, three decades later they were still able to work together on the setting up of the Irish Academy of Letters in 1932.

While lacking Yeats's spark of genius, A.E. was a gifted writer, who wrote poetry and mystical prose all his life. As a man of his times, A.E. was just as fascinating a figure as his more illustrious contemporary. Indeed, his life and work may well be more representative, and thus more revealing of the time and the place in which he lived. He was at the heart of Ireland's cultural, intellectual, and political life throughout the first three, transformative decades of the twentieth century.

The Poet

A.E.'s approach to poetry can be gauged from a review of Yeats's poems published in 1895 in which he praised his friend's work for being "full of the wisdom of the soul", "in kinship with elemental things", and "in alliance with the natural order". Elsewhere, he wrote of the "note of spirituality" and the lure of "that inner Ireland which has been the hearth and home of our mystic line of poets, where the eternal Ossianic murmur still sounds for those who listen". And there is indeed an otherworldly quality to his poetry so very different from the utilitarian pragmatism of his journalistic commentaries.

Throughout his life as a poet, A.E. followed unvarying precepts. From first to last he sought to win,

> *Rare vistas of white light,*
> *Half-parted lips through which the Infinite*
> *Murmurs its ancient story*

An early poem, "The Unknown God", captures the essence, and the preoccupations, of his poetry:

> *Far up the dim twilight fluttered*
>   *Moth-wings of vapour and flame:*
> *The lights danced over the mountains,*
>   *Star after star they came.*
>
> *The lights grew thicker unheeded,*
>   *For silent and still were we;*
> *Our hearts were drunk with a beauty*
>   *Our eyes could never see.*

His verse is replete with twilights and of the spiritual enchantments of the natural world.

While A.E.'s thinking evolved throughout a busy life, his poetry remained steadfast in its spiritual focus as in a later poem, "Ancient":

Out of a timeless world
Shadows fall upon Time,
From a beauty older than earth
A ladder the soul may climb.
I climb by the phantom stair
To a whiteness older than Time.

While not generally given to the kind of public poetry in which W.B. Yeats excelled, occasionally A.E. did allow his verse to take on a temporal voice as in his poem "On Behalf of Some Irishmen Not Followers of Tradition":

They call us aliens, we are told,
Because our wayward visions stray
From the dim banner they unfold,
The dreams of worn-out yesterday.

This work is reminiscent of Yeats's poem, "To Ireland in the Coming Times", where he aspires to "sweeten Ireland's wrong" while also insisting that "My rhymes more than their rhyming tell/Of things discovered in the deep".

Unusually, A.E.'s poem is more combative than Yeats's for he declares:

We would no Irish sign efface,
But yet our lips would gladlier hail
The firstborn of the Coming Race
Than the last splendour of the Gael.

Selected Poems

No blazoned banner we unfold—
One charge we give to youth,
Against the sceptred myth to hold
The golden heresy of truth.

The poem reflects the tension between the Gaelic and Anglo-Irish strands in Irish identity as it was squabbled over in the opening years of the twentieth century. A.E. was a target for D.P. Moran, the combative author of *The Philosophy of Irish Ireland*, who derided his Celtic spirituality and described the bearded, mystical A.E. as "the hairy fairy".

The most important public poem A.E. ever wrote had an awkward title, "To the Memory of Some I Knew Who Are Dead and Who Loved Ireland", and was published in 1917. Its outstanding feature is that it pays tribute not only to the leaders of the Easter Rising—Patrick Pearse, Thomas MacDonagh, James Connolly, and Constance Markievicz—but also to those who lost their lives during the First World War—Alan Anderson, the son of a colleague of A.E.'s in the cooperative movement, the former nationalist MP, Tom Kettle, and Willie Redmond MP, brother of Irish Party leader John Redmond. A.E.'s inclusiveness may now seem commonplace, but for most of the past hundred years it was nothing of the sort.

His final verse evokes "the confluence of dreams",

That clashed together in our night,
One river, born from many streams,
Roll in one blaze of blinding light.

The Seer

A.E.'s Celtic spirituality was an integral part of who he was. For him, the inner realm of the soul and natural world around him were intimately connected. There were "windows in the soul through which can be seen images created not by human but by the divine imagination". His visionary experiences came to him from "the true home of man", the visible world being "like a tapestry blown and stirred by the winds behind it." In his meditative work, *The Candle of Vision*, he describes how as a young man he "became aware of a mysterious life quickening within my life" in which "intense and passionate imaginations of another world, of an interior nature began to overpower me."

A.E. believed that he had found in late-nineteenth century Ireland "clear traces of that old wisdom-religion once universal". That old religion was founded on a belief that "life is one; that nature is not dead but living; the surface but a veil tremulous with light".

This vision of Ireland's special status as the home of unique spiritual values in a materialistic world was not unique to A.E. Yeats made equally lofty claims for ancient Ireland, which he saw as "one of the seven great fountains in the garden of the world's imagination." And what of Patrick Pearse with his high expectations for the Gael, who "is not like other men", but "the saviour of idealism", "the instructor of the nations", and "the preacher of the gospel of nature-worship"?

The more sober Thomas MacDonagh shared this idealistic sense of Ireland's past, and its destiny:

When the life of the cities of Europe goes
The way of Memphis and Babylon
In Ireland still the mystic rose
Will shine as it of old has shone.

When Russell enthused about "the awakening of the ancient fires" in modern Ireland, and when he wrote that "the Gods have returned to Erin and have centred themselves in the sacred mountains and blow the fires throughout the country", he was tapping into the spirit of that era in Ireland.

The Scribe

No other writer of significance can match A.E.'s record as an acute, intensive observer of the Ireland in which he lived. Unlike Yeats, who spent much of his life outside of Ireland, A.E. only rarely left his homeland, taking his holidays each summer in Donegal. His analysis of events in Ireland between the 1890s and the early 1930s is to be found in his contributions to the journals he edited, *The Irish Homestead* (1904-1923) and *The Irish Statesman* (1923-1930), and in a series of now-inaccessible books and pamphlets.

In a later work, *The Interpreters*, A.E. offered an account of his journey from a deeply personal mysticism to a profound romantic nationalism:

> I began to see in that interior light figures which enchanted me with their beauty. These were at first mythological in character and I could not connect them with anything in the world. Then I read the history of our nation, and I was excited by that tale which began among the gods, and from history I turned to literature, and it was then I knew that the forms I had seen in vision had been present to our ancestors thousands of years ago, and ever since they had been in the imaginations of the poets. I felt the continuity of national inspiration, that same light cast upon generation after generation . . .

A key turning point in A.E.'s life came in 1897 when Yeats recommended him to Horace Plunkett, who offered him a post with the nascent agricultural cooperative movement as a banks organiser. In this role, A.E. toured the west of Ireland extolling the virtues of cooperation. What he saw in rural Ireland depressed him. The living conditions he encountered were "a disgrace to humanity", but he was also charmed by stories of fairies he came across on his travels.

From the vantage point of his editorial desk at *The Irish Homestead*, he set out his vision for Ireland's future based on the principles of cooperation in which he passionately came to believe. He also published short stories by James Joyce, to whom he said, "Young man, there is not enough chaos in your mind". These stories subsequently became part of Joyce's collection, *Dubliners*. Joyce repaid A.E.'s literary patronage with some gentle mockery in *Ulysses* where he muses about his pen-name and the impact of vegetarianism on his ethereal poetry.

A.E. took a supportive interest in the plight of Dublin's workers during the lock-out of 1913, speaking and writing passionately on their behalf. He warned Dublin's employers that the restlessness and poverty of their employees was making "our industrial civilisation shake like a quaking bog". His sympathy for the workers brought him into contact with James Connolly, whose work he came to admire and whose influence he saw as paramount in bringing about the Easter Rising. A.E.'s conclusion was that the roots of the Rising lay in "the indifference of the wealthier to those in the social underworld". A lifelong pacifist, A.E. could not support the Rising, but he was moved by the ideals of its leaders.

In 1916, he published his lengthiest piece of political writing, *The National Being*, in which he produced an "imaginative meditation" on Ireland's "character and future". His aim was to "quicken the intellect and imagination of Ireland" and "to make the cooperative principle the basis of a national civilisation." By the time of the book's publication, however, events in Ireland had moved beyond the reach of A.E.'s reasoned analysis and his sober prose. He viewed with deepening foreboding Ireland's descent into violence and was depressed especially by attacks on cooperative premises. He took part in the Irish Convention of 1917-1918, an unsuccessful effort to reach political agreement between unionists and nationalists. When he resigned from the Convention in disgust at British Government promises to the Ulster Unionists, he nailed his colours to the mast: "A man must be either an Irishman or an Englishman in this matter. I am Irish."

During Ireland's war of independence, he increasingly sided with the Sinn Féin movement, but the outbreak of the Civil War pained him as it threatened to wreck the economic hopes he harboured for a self-governing Ireland. As editor of *The Irish Statesman*, A.E. had a ringside seat in the early years of the State's existence. When he launched this paper in 1923, he was full of hope for Ireland's future, but was also aware of the risk that the country's promise might be difficult to fulfil in the aftermath of a bitter civil war. In his first editorial, he looked for inspiration to the expansive, cultural nationalism that flourished in turn of the century Ireland.

> It is only too often true in the life of nations, as well as of individuals, that the dream or hope which precedes action is nobler than the realisation. If we are not to fail to realise our best aspirations we must recall to memory those ideals which made Ireland in pre-war days so intellectually interesting to ourselves and to other nations.

A.E. experienced deepening disenchantment during the 1920s as the realities of independence failed to live up to his hopes and expectations. The turning point for A.E. was the state imposition of censorship, which depressed his usually buoyant spirits. When *The Irish Statesman* folded in 1930, he began to spend more time outside of Ireland, including lecture tours of the United States where his ideas about rural life found favour in high places, including President Franklin Roosevelt.

By the early 1930s, A.E. would look back with sadness at the passing of a generation that was "a rarer and finer breed of life than those who came after" and at what he dismissed as a "half-crazy Gaeldom which is growing dominant about us." He left Ireland in 1933, having found himself "oversaturated with Irish ideas" and died in Bournemouth on 17 July 1935.

A.E. was a remarkable figure from an outstanding Irish generation, remarkable for the diversity of his achievements, as a poet, a painter, an accomplished editor, and a writer of books and pamphlets on mystical and political topics. The young visionary of the 1880s evolved into a practical thinker on economic and social issues, and became an astute, dedicated political commentator. Yet as he mulled over the affairs of Ireland from the era of Parnell to that of de Valera, he never ceased to be absorbed by what he called "the candle of vision". A.E. always aspired to "see into the life of things", as Wordsworth once wrote, but the Irish poet also constantly strove to put his stamp on the things of life.

Daniel Mulhall
London, 2017

Selected Bibliography

Writings by A.E.

Homeward, Songs by the Way
Dublin: Whaley & Co., 1894

The Earth Breath and Other Poems
London: John Lane, 1897

The Nuts of Knowledge
Dublin: Dun Emer Press, 1903

The Divine Vision and Other Poems
London: Macmillan and Co., 1904

The Mask of Apollo and Other Stories
Dublin: Whaley & Co., 1905

Deirdre: A Drama in Three Acts
Dublin: Maunsel & Co., 1907

Collected Poems
London: Macmillan and Co., 1913

Gods of War, with Other Poems
Dublin: Privately printed, 1915

Selected Poems

Imaginations and Reveries
Dublin: Maunsel & Co., 1915

The National Being:
Some Thoughts on an Irish Polity
Dublin: Maunsel & Co., 1916

The Candle of Vision
London: Macmillan and Co., 1918

The Interpreters
London: Macmillan and Co., 1922

Voices of the Stones
London: Macmillan and Co., 1925

Vale and Other Poems
London: Macmillan and Co., 1931

Song and Its Fountains
London: Macmillan and Co., 1932

The Avatars: A Futurist Fantasy
London: Macmillan and Co., 1933

The House of the Titans and Other Poems
London: Macmillan and Co., 1934

Selected Poems
London: Macmillan and Co., 1935

The Living Torch
Edited by Monk Gibbon
London: Macmillan and Co., 1937

Selected Bibliography

Further Reading

Alan, Nicholas. *George Russell (A.E.) and the New Ireland, 1905-30*. Dublin: Four Courts Press, 2004.

Clyde, William M. *A.E.* Edinburgh: The Morey Press, 1935.

Denson, Alan (ed). *Letters from A.E.* London: Abelard-Schuman, 1961.

Denson, Alan. *Printed Writings by George W. Russell (A.E.)*. Evanston: Northwestern University, 1961.

Eglinton, John. *A Memoir of A.E.* London: Macmillan, 1937.

Figgis, Darrell. *A.E.: A Study of a Man and a Nation*. Dublin: Maunsel & Co., 1916.

Kain, Richard M. and James H. O'Brien. *George Russell (A.E.)*. Lewisburg: Bucknell University, 1976.

Summerfield, Henry. *That Myriad-Minded Man*. Gerrards Cross: Colin Smythe, 1975.

Acknowledgements

The publisher would like to thank those who helped see this sesquicentenary edition of A.E.'s *Selected Poems* into publication: Meggan Kehrli, Ken Mackenzie, Bjorn Markeson, Daniel Mulhall, Jim Rockhill, and Colin Smythe.

Selected Poems was first published by
Macmillan and Company, London (1935).

"A Visionary" first appeared in
The Celtic Twilight by W. B. Yeats.
Lawrence and Bullen, London (1893).

"An Evening with A.E."
by Edgar DeWitt Jones first appeared in
The Christian Century, 20 April 1938.

"Poet, Seer and Scribe"
by Daniel Mulhall appears
here for the first time.

About the Author

George William Russell (1867-1935)—who published as "A.E."—was a poet, painter, economist, and mystic. In 1897 he started work with Sir Horace Plunkett's Irish Agricultural Organisation Society, editing their journal *The Irish Homestead*. In addition to numerous volumes of poetry, essays, and mystical writings, A.E. also nurtured the careers of Ireland's most important writers, including Patrick Kavanagh, James Stephens, and James Joyce. Highly regarded in life, on his death A.E.'s funeral cortège was over a mile long.

SWAN RIVER PRESS

Founded in 2003, Swan River Press is an independent publishing company, based in Dublin, Ireland, dedicated to gothic, supernatural, and fantastic literature. We specialise in limited edition hardbacks, publishing fiction from around the world with an emphasis on Ireland's contributions to the genre.

www.swanriverpress.ie

*"Handsome, beautifully made volumes . . .
altogether irresistible."*

– Michael Dirda, *Washington Post*

*"It [is] often down to small, independent, specialist presses
to keep the candle of horror fiction flickering . . . "*

– Darryl Jones, *Irish Times*

*"Swan River Press has emerged as one of the most inspiring
new presses over the past decade. Not only are the books
beautifully presented and professionally produced, but they
aspire consistently to high literary quality and originality,
ranging from current writers of supernatural/weird fiction
to rare or forgotten works by departed authors."*

– Peter Bell, *Ghosts & Scholars*

THE GREEN BOOK
*Writings on Irish Gothic,
Supernatural and Fantastic Literature*

edited by
Brian J. Showers

Aimed at a general readership and published twice-yearly, *The Green Book* features commentaries, articles, and reviews on Irish Gothic, Supernatural and Fantastic literature.

Certainly favourites such as Bram Stoker and John Connolly will come to mind, but *The Green Book* also showcases Ireland's other notable fantasists: Fitz-James O'Brien, Charlotte Riddell, Lafcadio Hearn, Rosa Mulholland, J. Sheridan Le Fanu, Cheiro, Harry Clarke, Dorothy Macardle, Lord Dunsany, Elizabeth Bowen, C. S. Lewis, Mervyn Wall, Conor McPherson . . . and many others.

*"A welcome addition to the realm of accessible
nonfiction about supernatural horror."*

– Ellen Datlow

*"Eminently readable . . . [an] engaging little journal
that treads the path between accessibility and
academic depth with real panache."*

– Peter Tenant, *Black Static*

THE DEATH SPANCEL
and Others

Katharine Tynan

Katharine Tynan is not a name immediately associated with the supernatural. However, like many other writers of the early twentieth century, she made numerous forays into literature of the ghostly and macabre, and throughout her career produced verse and prose that conveys a remarkable variety of eerie themes, moods, and narrative forms. From her early, elegiac stories, inspired by legends from the West of Ireland, to pulpier efforts featuring grave-robbers and ravenous rats, Tynan displays an eye for weird detail, compelling atmosphere, and a talent for rendering a broad palette of uncanny effects. *The Death Spancel and Others* is the first collection to showcase Tynan's tales of supernatural events, prophecies, curses, apparitions, and a pervasive sense of the ghastly.

"Of remarkably high literary quality . . . a great collection recommended to any good fiction lover."

– Mario Guslandi

"Tynan's fiction is of a high standard, crafted in relatively simple yet still lyrical prose . . . a very assured craftswoman of the supernatural tale."

– Supernatural Tales

"Lovers of late Victorian and Edwardian ghost fiction will assuredly adore the restrained literary quality . . ."

– The Pan Review

EARTH-BOUND
and Other Supernatural Tales

Dorothy Macardle

Originally published in 1924, the nine tales that comprise Earth-Bound were written by Dorothy Macardle while she was held a political prisoner in Dublin's Kilmainham Gaol and Mountjoy Prison. The stories incorporate themes that intrigued her throughout her life; themes out of the myths and legends of Ireland; ghostly interventions, dreams and premonitions, clairvoyance, and the Otherworld in parallel with this one. It is so easy to dismiss them, as some have, merely as part of the narrative of "Irish nationalism" of the time, but it is the supernatural elements that make them much more. She would revisit these themes in later works such as her classic haunted house novel *The Uninvited* (1941). To this new edition of Macardle's debut collection, reprinted for the first time in ninety years, we have added four more tales of the supernatural.

"Beautifully written, with a fine air for the music of language and vivid descriptions of the landscape."

– Black Static

"A beautifully presented and valuable resource for anyone interested in Irish history, culture or literature."

– Dublin Inquirer

www.ingramcontent.com/pod-product-compliance
Lightning Source LLC
Chambersburg PA
CBHW020904080526
44589CB00011B/436